Pay ♡ W9-BRN-455

Reluctant Disciplinarian

Advice on classroom management from a softy who became (eventually) a successful teacher

Gary Rubinstein

illustrated by Larry Nolte

PRUFROCK PRESS INC.
WACO, TEXAS

Copyright ©2010, Prufrock Press Inc.

ISBN-13: 978-1-936162-15-4

No part of this book may be reproduced, translated, stored in a retrieval system, or transmitted, in any form or by any means, electronic, mechanical, photocopying, microfilming, recording, or otherwise, without written permission from the publisher.

For more information about our copyright policy or to request reprint permissions, visit https://www.prufrock.com/permissions.aspx.

Printed in the United States of America.

At the time of this book's publication, all facts and figures cited are the most current available; all telephone numbers, addresses, and website URLs are accurate and active; all publications, organizations, websites, and other resources exist as described in this book; and all have been verified. The author(s) and Prufrock Press make no warranty or guarantee concerning the information and materials given out by organizations or content found at websites, and we are not responsible for any changes that occur after this book's publication. If you find an error or believe that a resource listed here is not as described, please contact Prufrock Press.

Prufrock Press Inc.
P.O. Box 8813
Waco, TX 76714-8813
Phone: (800) 998-2208
Fax: (800) 240-0333
http://www.prufrock.com

For my parents

Table of Contents

The Accidental Teacher

Not every motive is a "pure" motive

The Accidental Teacher

Until I was 21, I never gave much thought to the question, "What do you want to be when you grow up?" My mother always said I would be a lawyer, so who was *I* to argue?

As my college had no pre-law program, I majored in the subject I liked most: math. But as graduation neared and law school applications cluttered my dorm room desk, I realized that I didn't want to study law. I was tired of writing papers and listening to lectures. Rather than learn more about life, I was ready to live. Living, however, required finding a job and deciding on a city in which to live.

My friend Eric, who was having similar reservations about law school, presented me with a flyer for the one-year-old Teach For America program. Teach For America (TFA) recruits recent college graduates — ones who have *not* majored in education — to teach in rural and inner-city schools throughout the country. Like a domestic Peace Corps, TFA members commit to serving for two years wherever TFA places them. The philosophy is that these non-career teachers will become lifelong supporters of public schools after they go on to pursue other careers.

I felt I had an aptitude for teaching.

"It will be great," Eric assured me. "We'll both move down to someplace like Mississippi. We'll live by the school in a cheap apartment, get to know everyone in town, and teach the kids."

For me this was the perfect diversion. I was not a stranger to teaching, having worked as a math tutor since I was a junior in high school and also, for two years during college, as an instructor for an SAT preparation course. I enjoyed teaching and felt I had an aptitude for it. By joining TFA I could do something good for society while simultaneously getting someone else to tell me where to live and where to work.

Eric never applied. TFA was just a passing whim for him, but he had made it sound so appealing that I decided to apply anyway. Though the application was reminiscent of the law school applications I had just discarded, I considered it a good omen that I found the "Why do you want to teach?" essay much easier to write than its "Why do you want to be a lawyer?" counterpart.

That summer, I was off to the TFA summer institute, a seven week "boot camp" for new teachers. At the institute I met an incredible assortment of people. Talking with some of them, I was often intimidated by their passion. Most people who join an organization like TFA, I learned, do it for very "good" reasons: They want to give back to the system that provided them with a college education. They want to influence the lives of needy children. They want to make a difference.

Hearing my fellow corps members speak so intensely about working to combat the injustices of the American educational system, I began to worry that my motives were not pure enough. I knew that I was doing it not only to save children, but also to save myself.

Partly because I was too lazy to fill out my law school applications, I took on the most difficult challenge I had ever faced. Partly because I was not ready to take on the responsibility of finding a job and choosing a place to live, I took on an even greater responsibility — the responsibility of educating children.

I took on the most difficult challenge I had ever faced.

History of a Softy

It's not easy being mean

History of a Softy

Knowing that how well you do something is at least as important as why you choose to do it, I worked hard to learn as much as I could at the demanding TFA institute. Mornings, we did our student teaching. Afternoons, we met with institute faculty, an amazing hand-picked team of mentors from across the country. Evenings, we read up on educational methodology and planned and graded for the following day. I learned as much as a person can learn about teaching in a short two months.

One of the topics I studied was discipline. I had reason to suspect that it was not going to be one of my biggest strengths.

A shaky start. My first experience as a disciplinarian came when I was five years old. I was helping my father housebreak the family dog, a Great Dane named Smokey.

Each time Smokey urinated on the living room plants, we would punish him. My father would drag the dog to the yellow puddle and begin by hitting, then screaming at him. After Dad was finished, I would go over to the dog and pat his head, telling Smokey that he was a good boy and that I loved him. As a result of my sympathy, it took years for the dog to stop vandalizing our home.

The first time I commanded a schoolroom was five years later when I was in the fourth grade. My teacher left the room, placing me, the class treasurer, in charge. My instructions were simple: While the class worked on a math assignment, I was to write down the names of anyone who talked.

Five minutes after the teacher left, a boy called me to his desk. "How do you do this one?" he asked. While I was helping him, two girls on the other side of the room began conversing. I speedily wrote their names on my "snitch paper." One of the girls noticed and immediately protested.

"If you write our names, you have to write his name too," she said, referring to the boy I was helping.

"That's different," I said. "He was asking me for help."

"Well, I was asking *her* for help," she responded. "It's the same thing."

Several others entered the argument. The consensus was that I should either write all three names or none of the names on the list. I disagreed, explaining that I would leave the two girls' names and add the names of those who had spoken in the girls' defense.

The students continued to argue that my name should go on the list as well, since I was also talking. Unable to respond intelligently to such logic, I allowed the class to manipulate me into writing down my own name. When the teacher returned, I sheepishly handed her the list and went

back to my seat. The conspicuous appearance of my name
on the paper invalidated its credibility, so no one got in
trouble.

From my early years, my natural tendency has always
been to be an overly sympathetic softy whom students could
easily manipulate. And with that trait, I began my student
teaching in the summer of 1991.

Student teaching with Ms. Kowalski. Having heard
how difficult junior high students can be, I had requested a
student teaching assignment in a high school. Instead I was
sent to an urban junior high in California.

My mentor was a teacher named Ms. Kowalski, a strict
disciplinarian. Her strategy was to train her students like
dogs. Following her lead, I treated them like dogs too — just
like Smokey. When Ms. Kowalski would yell at a student,
reducing him to tears, I would soon be patting him on the
back and telling him not to worry.

In front of the class, I didn't have many discipline problems. If a student got out of hand, I would merely say, "I'm
telling Ms. Kowalski," and he would immediately behave.
At my going-away party, the students gave me a standing
ovation when the principal presented me with an honorary
diploma. After he left, Ms. Kowalski yelled at one of the
girls for cheering too loudly. The girl began to cry, and I,
of course, consoled her. Six weeks of training had not hard-
ened my classroom persona. I was still a marshmallow.

I was about to be roasted.

My first teaching job. After student teaching, I got a job
at a middle school in a large city. I was screaming at students
by the end of the first week.

*With
Ms. Kowalski
around,
I didn't have
many discipline
problems.*

11

*In one month,
I went from
"Please be
respectful of
others" to
"Shut up!"*

My requests for silence quickly went from "Please be respectful of others" to "Please be quiet" to "Be quiet." Later it was "Shhh," then "Shush," then "Shush up," and finally "Shut up!" In a last desperate effort to gain control, I warned them, "I'm telling Ms. Kowalski."

Once when I was absent, my class tortured the substitute. They set a fire in the garbage can. They threw some books out the window. When I returned the next day, I reprimanded them harshly. "Why can't you be that good for me?" I asked.

During my first year, I was hit by students on three different occasions. Rather than expel students for something that was a result of my incompetence, school officials made what is called a "disciplinary exchange" with another school. One time they traded a chronic truant and a student who had hit me for two graffiti artists and a delinquent to be named later.

A stronger second year. By my second year of teaching, I had learned a few things. I had learned that any time a teacher makes a blanket threat such as, "The next student who talks is getting detention," the first one to break the silence will be the quietest student in the class. (It is tempting to say, instead, "The next *bad* student who talks is getting detention.")

I had learned to implement logical consequences, making punishment more meaningful by relating it to the crime: If the students threw paper, I made them clean the room. If they came late, I made them stay after class. If they talked too much, I made an appointment for them to meet with the mutual funds salesman who camped in my staff lounge.

Additionally, I had learned to mask any remaining softness with the "teacher look." My look became so effective that I could quiet crying babies on airplanes or silence obnoxious people sitting behind me at the movies. (My most powerful look I reserved for halting volcanoes and other natural disasters.)

A successful third year. By the end of my third year of teaching, I was doing fine. I had made the difficult transformation from born pushover to real teacher. In my fourth year, I was even named Teacher of the Year at my school.

Was I an expert? No. However, I had learned a lot in my struggle to learn effective classroom management. Most important, I had learned how to make my classroom a place where students could be successful.

*Eventually,
I made the
transformation
from born
pushover to real
teacher.*

Why Learning to Discipline Is So Hard

Traditional methods of teaching classroom management just don't work

Why Learning to Discipline Is So Hard

Like many teachers, I had a hard time learning classroom management. Learning to discipline is difficult, and traditional methods of teaching it are not generally very successful.

Most teachers try to learn classroom management with one of the following methods:

1. Taking education courses
2. Observing good teachers
3. Student teaching
4. Taking in-service classes
5. Learning from mistakes

Each of these methods, unfortunately, is flawed in its own unique way. Consequently, too many teachers struggle through their first year, expending vast quantities of energy trying to maintain classroom discipline — at the expense of teaching.

Taking education courses

Education courses are widely viewed as "fluff."

Most teachers agree that the training they received in college did not prepare them adequately for the realities of the classroom. Education courses typically consist of either (a) a lot of abstract theory, often taught by professors who haven't been in a public school classroom in years, if ever, or (b) classes that are widely viewed as "fluff," with little real content. Ironically, these are the same courses that usually contain the advice that future teachers should always maintain high expectations of their students.

Too often, the excuse offered for ineffective education courses is, "You can't really teach somebody how to teach." As a math teacher, I doubt that I would keep my job very long if I went around saying, "You can't teach somebody how to do math."

Outside of teaching, I have worked at many other jobs, ranging from "ice cream man" to "software engineer." Of all the jobs, teaching has been the most challenging in every way, including intellectually. It only makes sense that such a difficult occupation should demand more difficult training. (You never hear soldiers laughing about how easy they had it in boot camp.)

*The difficult
occupation
of teaching
should demand
more difficult
training.*

Education courses?

College education courses have a poor reputation. They are all too often described as mindless courses with little content. They are looking more and more like the following:

ED 117
Bulletin boards

Learn the fundamentals of conceiving, designing and implementing innovative bulletin boards. Answer the age-old question, "Staples or thumb tacks: Which address more modalities?" Learn the difference between specific and universal themes. Why create a design that will be obsolete in a few days when you can make a bulletin board like "Be Proud to Be You" that will last the entire year?

ED 079
Class pets

Learn how introducing a class pet into your elementary classroom can teach students about responsibility. (Get two pets, and incorporate sex education into your lesson plan.) If a pet dies, lead an emotional class discussion on the meaning of life and death. Dissection can also be studied at this time.

ED 051
Time management
for teachers

Learn how to maximize planning time and eliminate mountains of paperwork. Hours can be saved by letting students mark their own papers. Keeping them honest is just a matter of saying, "I'm going to re-check all of these myself, so don't try to cheat." Learn to say this without giggling. Master the incredible "check system" of grading a set of 35 papers in just two minutes. Delve into the controversial technique of "throwing away papers." Related topic: "Giving Scantron Essay Tests."

ED 199
Reverse psychology

You wouldn't like this course, so forget about it. It's probably too hard for you anyway.

ED 282
Basic photocopy machine repair

Learn how to handle common photocopy machine malfunctions, including paper jams, empty ink cartridges and misfeeds. Learn how most problems can be fixed by simply switching the machine off and then back on again. Learn coping techniques, like just leaving the machine so that the next person thinks *she* broke it. Related topic: Copying "Out of Order" signs — Do it *before* the machine breaks.

ED 211
Seminar in urban education

Classes will discuss the shortcomings of public education. The classic text *Why Johnny Can't Read* will be studied, along with its frightening sequel, *Why Johnny Can't Factor Quadratic Polynomials*.

Observing good teachers

*Good teachers
make classroom
management
look dangerously
easy.*

As part of the training process, future teachers are often sent to observe dynamic teachers. They scribble notes furiously, as these phenomenons silence chatter by merely asking, "Are you respecting your classmates right now?"

After observing one teacher with excellent classroom control, I asked, "What do you do if they throw paper airplanes?" She answered, immediately, "I don't put up with that kind of nonsense!" In my notebook, I jotted, "Don't put up with that kind of nonsense!"

The problem with observing and interviewing good teachers is that they don't have big discipline problems. They make management look dangerously easy. Observing them can lead to overconfidence in unsuspecting novices.

New or future teachers leave a mentor's room delighted with their new collection of foolproof ideas, which they have just witnessed working flawlessly. To assume that these ideas will automatically work for less experienced teachers is like assuming that any golfer can clear the water hole with a five-iron from 200 yards, just because he has seen Tiger Woods do it on television.

Student teaching

By my third week as a student teacher, I was in charge of instruction. Ms. Kowalski would sit at her desk, silently maintaining order with her presence. I could turn my back to write on the board, confident that she would serve as the eyes in the back of my head. (She assured me that I would eventually develop my own.)

I was aware that this scenario was artificial, merely a weak simulation of how things would be with my own class. Although she would sometimes leave the room for a few minutes, the students knew that at any moment she could pop in the door or spy through the window. I needed for her to be absent, but her presence each morning was as consistent as the sun's.

Most student teachers teach in similar circumstances. No matter what, the student teacher and the students themselves all recognize that the student teacher is not the "real" teacher.

Students everywhere recognize that the student teacher is not the "real" teacher.

Life without Ms. Kowalski. When I was student teaching, I at last got the opportunity to shine in the absence of Ms. Kowalski. Her absence occurred on the same day as another once-in-a-century event — a total solar eclipse. It was the perfect opportunity to test my theory of discipline: that a teacher with exciting lessons doesn't need to be a strong disciplinarian. What student would misbehave while witnessing such a rare celestial event?

My roommate had taught me how to make an eclipse viewer with a piece of construction paper and a pin. When I told the substitute, a friendly woman in her early thirties,

The substitute sat in the back of the room, reading a novel.

about my plans to make viewers and take the students outside to view the eclipse, she vetoed the idea. She claimed that staring at the eclipse was dangerous and that she would be held responsible if a student went blind.

I explained to my class that because Ms. Kowalski wasn't there to supervise, we couldn't go outside. The students begged and pleaded. Finally, a girl named Carolina called out, in panic, "But, Mr. Rubinstein, it's not going to happen again for another 125 years."

I didn't have the heart to say, "In that case, you'll really appreciate the next one." I had to say something, though, and it had to be decisive.

"I'll ask the principal," I said. I sprinted outside, found him and got his approval. Frantically, we began constructing the eclipse viewers, poking holes in construction paper with a borrowed earring because we didn't have pins.

Soon I had the class lined up single file. "Don't look at the sky," I barked. "Look at your shadow." We sidestepped our way north, like some kind of chorus line, toward the football field. There we held up our papers and examined the shadow, watching intently.

It worked. Hypnotized by the strange growing crescent in the hole of the viewer's shadow, the students stared safely at the evolving shape for the rest of the period.

Total eclipse of the sub. Amazingly, Ms. Kowalski was again missing the next day. In her place was a new sub, a large young man who sat at the desk reading a hardback novel. He didn't seem to want interruptions, so I went directly to the front of the room and began teaching, without introducing myself.

The students seemed more energetic, calling out answers and chattering, I hoped, about the lesson. When the noise got too loud, I had an opportunity to try my "respect" speech: "You'll have to keep it down. Please show respect for me, for your classmates, and most importantly, for yourselves." The following silence was shorter than the speech.

In the middle of the period, at a particular crescendo, the sub stood and screamed, "Shut up!" The students were quiet for the rest of the period.

When the bell to start second period sounded that day, Eddie, one of the toughest students in the class, was running toward the room to get to class on time. The substitute slammed the door and locked it, while Eddie banged at the door and screamed. When I went to open the door, the sub said, "Let him bang for a while. Next time he'll be on time."

When the noise got too loud, I had an opportunity to try my "respect" speech.

I let Eddie in anyway. He walked up to the sub and said, "Man, why'd you slam the door in my face?"

The sub yelled his response: "Don't you take that tone with me. You're going to the office."

The class looked at me.

"No, he's not," I said calmly. "He's going to his seat."

*Oversimplified
beliefs can lead
to a false sense
of confidence.*

The sub then yelled at me, "Who's in charge here? You or me?"

"Let me tell you something," I said. "I'm not an aide and I'm not a sub. I'm a teacher, and I've been teaching this class by myself for the past three weeks. I handle my own discipline problems in class, so he's not going to the office. He's going to his seat where he has a chance to learn some math."

Eddie went to his seat and was silent for the entire period, along with everyone else in the room, including the sub.

A false lesson learned. My eclipse lesson seemed to prove that students will behave if they are permitted to learn and have fun at the same time. My triumph over the mean substitute seemed to prove that teachers can be kind and respectful and still keep control of their classes.

However, these oversimplified beliefs only served to give me a false sense of confidence in my abilities, leading to many problems when I was finally in charge of a class of my own.

I had thought Ms. Kowalski's two-day absence had turned me into a real teacher. I was wrong.

Taking in-service classes

School in-service classes are times of role reversal: Teachers become students (loud and uncooperative). Administrators become teachers (boring and demanding). Students become administrators (at home sleeping). Unfortunately, the typical in-service rarely provides anything valuable.

In-service topics range from the utterly useless to the totally useless.

In-service topics range from the utterly useless to the totally useless. One year my colleagues and I spent three hours learning the subtleties of new grade sheets, with advice like, "When you bubble, use a number two pencil, and be sure to erase any stray marks." At my friend's school, teachers recently received "risk management" training. This program could have been called "How to avoid hurting yourself on campus so we don't have to pay your disability income," with advice like, "You can prevent slipping on rainy days by thoroughly drying off your shoes when going indoors."

If a television is posted near the podium, teachers can be sure they are about to endure the least effective in-service imaginable — the video. I resent this medium because it just encourages those teachers who too often elect to "make it a Blockbuster lesson." The video usually depicts a round-table informational meeting with a group of teachers asking the moderator about the in-service topic. The video, with its bad acting and unnatural dialogue, takes the tone of a late-night infomercial.

Sometimes teachers are given an information packet to supplement the video. Once, while watching a video describing the latest standardized test, I flipped through the booklet and discovered a section titled "Commonly Asked Questions." The questions and answers seemed very familiar. I soon discovered that they had given us the very script from which the teachers on the video were reading. I quickly pointed this out to some of the more obnoxious members of our staff, and they began reading the answers, loudly, along with the video. Others joined in, and soon there were nearly 20 teachers participating in the mockery.

It is not helpful to have a presenter lecture for an hour about how ineffective it is to lecture for an hour.

If no videotape is available, there is usually an "experienced" in-service presenter. The presenter at a session I once attended offered this instructional tip: "Don't just lecture the kiddos on Africa. Have them bring in African artifacts."

No in-service would be complete without a giant pad on which brainstorming results can be recorded. Ideas always look silly on those giant papers. There's a law of physics, I think: The importance of an idea is inversely proportional to the size of the paper on which it is written.

There are two main in-service presentation strategies. The first type is "the paradox." With the paradox

strategy, the presenter lectures for an hour about how ineffective it is to lecture for an hour.

More popular is "the demonstration method." With this
strategy, the presenter proves the effectiveness of various
teaching methods by using them to teach the teachers. For
example, the presenter may demonstrate a way to silence
a classroom. "Clap once if you can hear me," she says. A
few people clap. "Clap twice if you can hear me." Half the
people clap twice. "Clap three times of you can hear me."
The entire faculty claps three times and waits quietly. The
presenter then nods her head and flashes an irritating grin.

On paper, the "clap" method makes sense: Students will
quiet their voices as they make a specific noise. Unfortunately,
real students do not live on paper. My first year, I attempted
the "clap" strategy with one of my classes. To this day, some
of those students are still clapping.

Just because a lesson works for a room full of teachers
acting like students does not mean it will work for a room
full of real students acting like students. When teachers
try to act like real students, we inadvertently act like *paper*
students. This is because we don't know what real students
think. If we did, we wouldn't need teacher in-service days in
the first place.

Since I won't try to act like a student at in-services, I
normally sit and do nothing. Ironically, by refusing to participate, I am acting like a real student. If they can teach me
something while I'm in that defiant frame of mind, then
their lesson may have merit.

Though they fail to educate teachers, school in-services
do unintentionally achieve something significant. They
remind both teachers and administrators how difficult it is
to sit on the other side of the desk. By dealing with rude

*Just because
a lesson works
for a room
full of teachers
acting like
students
does not mean
it will work
for a room
full of
real students
acting like
students.*

*School
in-services
remind teachers
how difficult
it is to sit on
the other side of
the desk.*

teachers, administrators remember how it feels to be a teacher. Teachers experience how difficult it is to sit there, uninvolved, wishing the time away.

Each time I leave an in-service, I vow to never subject my students to similar boredom. In that way, and in only that way, every in-service I have attended has helped make me a better teacher.

Learning from mistakes

The last way teachers find out about classroom management is probably the most common — by learning from their mistakes.

New teachers quickly learn that phrases their supervising teachers used so successfully do not contain any magic powers. Neither do the methods they observed master teachers using.

Soon new teachers begin fumbling and experimenting on their own, trying to find something that works. Though many great teachers have learned classroom management by such experimentation, the method has a serious drawback: It makes students the guinea pigs. Why should students suffer through a miserable year while their teacher figures out what to do?

New teachers discover quickly that what works for experienced teachers may not work for them.

An effective alternative

*Teachers
can learn by
analyzing
the mistakes
of others.*

There is an effective alternative to the five traditional methods of learning classroom management. That alternative is to learn from someone *else's* mistakes.

How often do teachers get to witness a totally out of control classroom? Rarely, if ever. Yet it is only by observing such a spectacle that teachers can truly appreciate how important discipline is. And only by analyzing the mistakes that lead to such chaos can new teachers learn what to avoid in their own classrooms.

But what pitiful teacher going through an awful year would actually let anyone observe him? Who could handle such ruthless scrutiny? What self-respecting teacher would look back on a teaching experience he so wished to forget, and then allow his mistakes to be dissected and held under a microscope — just so others could learn from them?

That teacher, sadly, is me.

What Does NOT Work

Most discipline tactics work
only if a class is already
somewhat under control

What Does NOT Work

I began my first year of teaching with little concern about discipline. I didn't *want* to have the total control some teachers boasted about having. I wanted my students to feel comfortable expressing themselves. My goal was for them to learn, not for them to be silent. If making a little noise would help them to learn more, that was fine with me.

Because of movies I had seen, like *Dangerous Minds*, I thought the first few days of the school year would be the most difficult. Get past those, I thought, and the rest of the year would be a snap.

I was thrilled when the first week of school turned out to be surprisingly easy. What I didn't realize, of course, was that the first few days of school are *usually* easy. Teachers fondly call this time the honeymoon period. It begins the first minute of the school year and ends when the teacher, while trying to silence the class, first plaintively utters the phrase, "Come on guys."

An easy first day does not mean an easy first year.

COME ON, GUYS...

If a little noise is supposed to help students learn more, it was soon apparent that, based on the commotion coming from my room, students in my class were going to be geniuses. Occasionally one student would start a chain reaction by singing a low "aah," slowly rising in pitch and volume. Within seconds, the entire class would be "ahhing" louder and higher, like a fire truck. I still have nightmares about that sight — the students with their mouths wide open, heads tilted back like Charlie Brown and friends during a sing-along. One day, each time I turned to write on the board, my entire class banged out the introduction to "We Will Rock You." Boom-Boom-Clap. Boom-Boom-Clap. Boom-Boom-Clap.

When teachers talk about their bad first year, they usually describe 15 minutes or so of chaos in the classroom. Unfortunately, a school year consists of an additional 49,485 minutes. The true flavor of first-year misery can only be appreciated by examining some of those average minutes.

One day when I was giving a lesson, for example, a student captured a typical moment of my first year. I noticed that Kimberly was writing at a furious pace. Since she was writing words instead of numbers, I assumed that she was writing a note to a friend and confiscated the note.

Then I saw that she actually *had* been taking notes. In fact, she was writing down every word I said. Here's what she had written:

*My classroom
was out of
control.*

*O.K. well Amber pay attention then you don't
have to move it add zeros if needed wait let me
get the eraser have you seen the eraser oh here it is
quiet quiet Erica Jaime quiet
Jaime quiet O.K. these are
very very easy O.K. number
one is opposite O.K. lets go
over these examples Jaime
you say that Jaime enough
of that when we watch the
TV your going to be sent to
Harper's room that's it that
is the answer don't write on
this keep your mouth shut
can we just write the answer
then Julio number three lets
talk about Julio the me guys
quiet Jaime three steps.*

Yes, my classroom was out of control. What was I to do about it?

**One student's record of my exact words during
an out-of-control class period**

Incremental consequences

*Using
incremental
consequences
in a chaotic
classroom is like
trying to slay a
dragon with a
fly swatter.*

In trying to solve my discipline problem, I thought back to what I had been taught in school during classes, observations and student teaching. One piece of advice I had heard was, "Use incremental consequences." These consequences were:

- Issuing warnings
- Writing names on the board
- Giving detention
- Sending to the office

I hadn't paid a lot of attention to this advice because I never thought I would need it. My style in life leaned more toward passive-aggressive methods like cold shoulders and guilt trips. Still, when things in my classroom degenerated into chaos, I tried using these consequences. That's when I realized that these tactics work in only one set of circumstances: when a class is already at least somewhat under control. Trying the consequences on the types of problems that I was dealing with was more like trying to slay a dragon with a fly swatter.

Besides, each consequence has problems associated with it.

Issuing warnings. The problem with warnings is that, if your class is out of control, it is almost impossible to keep track of who has a warning and who doesn't before you proceed to the second consequence — writing names on the board. When you do write a student's name on the board, he will say, "You didn't even give me a warning. No fair."

Unfortunately, sometimes I would get fed up with all the warnings and start skipping directly to step two, in which case I would be correctly accused of being unfair.

*Writing too
many names
on the board
can become
a great visual
joke.*

Writing names on the board. When a teacher writes only one or two names on the board, the action may have some impact. But after a certain number, writing names on the board becomes a great visual joke.

In my case, all the names maniacally scratched on the board revealed my frustration. Originally I reserved a spot on the side of the board for them, but I got tired of continually stopping and walking over there. To save time, I started writing the names wherever I happened to be standing. As a result, names were randomly scrawled all over the board. When I needed more space for the math examples, I had to carefully erase around the names. Sometimes, at the end of the period, two students would distract me with a fake fight

Discipline Quiz

thatthatthatthatthatthatthatthatthatthatthatthatthatthatthatthat-
that

while someone ran up and erased all the names from the board.

Between warnings and writing names on the board, I wasted at least half of every period — and that was before anyone suffered any real consequences.

Giving detention. I used to think the threat of detention would be a good deterrent. That was before I learned that, like many schools, mine had a reasonable rule about detention. Teachers have to give students one day's notice so that they can arrange for safe transportation home. Unfortunately, this delay means that students are not really affected by this type of detention because they have no sense of future. Telling a student that she has detention tomorrow is like telling her she will have detention eight years from last Wednesday.

When you give a student detention, you are giving yourself detention as well.

Sometimes I would get so frustrated that I would say, "The next person who talks is getting a week of detention." Since students have no sense of future, someone would always talk and I would have to follow through and stay after school monitoring detention for a full week. When you give a student detention, I learned, you are giving yourself detention as well.

What Does NOT Work

With a class as out of control as mine, it was impossible to keep track of all my threats.

Making threats. I soon realized that if I followed my consequence list too literally, most of the class would be in the office by the end of each period. Deciding that I would have to pace myself, I added a new step: making threats.

It was soon apparent that the problem with a threat is that it is just another warning. If one student gets a threat between detention and the next consequence, all students should get that same threat. However, with a class as out of control as mine, it was impossible to keep track of all the threats.

A common threat I used was the threat of a phone call to the student's parents. "One more word out of you, and I'm calling home tonight," I would say. This threat was ineffective for any or all of the following eight reasons:

1. The student didn't care if I called the parents.

2. The student liked to *pretend* that he didn't care if I called his parents.

3. The student's parents didn't have a phone.

4. The student's parents had a phone, but the student didn't live with his parents.

5. The student's parents had a phone, and the student lived with his parents, but the number he gave on his information card at the beginning of the year was actually the number for Blockbuster Video.

The threat of a phone call home to parents is rarely effective.

6. The student's parents had a phone, the student lived with his parents, and he had given me the correct number. However, when I called, he would intercept the phone and tell me that his parents weren't home.

7. The student's parents had a phone, the student lived with his parents, and he had given me the correct number. However, when I called, he put his older cousin on the phone to imitate his parents. If the student had a deep enough voice, he might even do the impersonation himself.

8. The student's parents had a phone, the student lived with his parents, he had given me the correct number, and his parents answered the phone. However, the parents wouldn't do anything to help, despite my call.

No matter what the reason, I found that the threat of a parental call is rarely effective.

Sending to the office. Sending a student to the office does not always have the effect we think it will. The assistant principal's office, in the first school where I taught, was like a private club for cool students. I once intercepted a note that read, "Try to get sent to the office during sixth period. I'll meet you there." In the office area, while waiting to see one of the assistant principals, a student would have fun talking and joking around and complaining that she wasn't "the only one doing it."

The assistant principal's office was a private club for cool students.

When you send someone to the office, in most schools, you have to stop class to write up a referral. In my school, I had to get a discipline card, write up a brief description of the offenses and then give the card to the student to bring with him to the assistant principal, who, after seeing the student, would fill out and return the bottom portion to me like a sales receipt. When I would hand the discipline card to the student, he would usually read it out loud to the class, and then announce, "You lie!" before storming out.

One discipline card I've saved reads:

1. Left room without permission.
2. Entered room through windows.
3. Was returned to class after conference with Gonzales and continued to cause trouble, throw SPITBALLS, change seats without permission, etc.

If the office was swarming with kids, the student would usually be gone for the rest of the period, which was fine with me. However, the bell served as a sort of statute of limitations. If the assistant principal didn't get to see a student before the bell rang, the infraction was ignored. My receipt might then read, "Not in office when I called for her."

If the office was *not* swarming with kids, the student would usually be back in class ten minutes later, wearing a big grin and announcing, "They didn't do nuthin.'" At the end of the day, I would receive a receipt that read, "Please be consistent. Send down all students guilty of the same offense, or none at all." Once it said, "Maybeline — Was she also shooting rubber bands? If so, you should send her to office also. Be fair always." I would often plead with this administrator, "I can only send down the people I *catch*."

The bell served as a sort of statute of limitations.

45

Yelling. They warned me in teacher training, "Whatever you do, don't yell." I wasn't worried. In my life, I had never raised my voice.

After a short time teaching, however, I had exhausted all other options. "Don't yell" sounded like other morsels of counter-intuitive advice I knew: Never scratch a poison ivy rash. If you're skidding on ice, don't hit the brakes. If you're in the ocean with a shark, stay still.

Losing control of your class is one thing; losing control of yourself is worse.

I quickly decided, enough of this advice. Enough of my life-long pursuit of passive resistance. Just give me peace and "QUIIEEEEEEEET!"

After my first shout, the class stared at me quietly. Some students were grinning. That first silence lasted about five minutes. Though I knew my students and I would likely become addicted to my yelling, requiring stronger stuff as we built our immunity, at that moment I did not care. What mattered was that I had finally found something that worked.

I soon established different levels of voice raising for different situations. I had to carefully choose from my arsenal. Too weak would not be heard. Too strong would make students laugh.

- The first level was shouting. This was most effective for small groups of talkers. A shout could gain up to two minutes of peace.

- Yelling, my most popular weapon, was the next level. During a yell, my voice would change slightly, but it would still be recognizable as mine. While yelling, I was still capable of saying full sentences. A yell would be good for about three minutes.

- Screaming was the next caliber. When I screamed, my voice would change pitch and character, as if I was possessed by Grover from *Sesame Street*. Screaming earned me four minutes of solace.

- The final level was hysterical screaming. I discovered this technique during my second period class when I left the room to investigate a suspicious boom in the hallway. While I was gone, the majority of the class started pounding loudly on their desks. I ran back into the room and, for some reason I don't quite understand myself, lifted a desk off the ground with a student in it. Unsure what to do with the desk, I put it and the student down and began screaming hysterically. I screamed at a level summoned from a section of my adrenal gland, a level previously reserved for warning loved ones they are in the path of an oncoming train.

Yelling quickly loses its effectiveness.

Hysterical screaming was effective, in the short run, for several reasons. Primarily, it quieted students because it was entertaining — hysterical in both senses of the word. My eyes would bulge, my glasses would fog and my curly hair would flop around. If nothing else, the screaming would at least signal teachers from nearby rooms to come to my rescue. The hysterical scream would get me about five minutes of silence, which was also the interval of time it took for me to recover from using it.

My worst episode was in the spring of my first year. With 20 minutes left in my fourth period class, the fire alarm sounded and we went outside. As I tried to maintain control of my class among the 2500 other students on the field in front of the school, I learned that the alarm signalled a real fire. The dean of instruction's office was

*If I screamed
as intensely as
I felt, I would
collapse.*

destroyed, though the fire had been quickly extinguished. The police and fire departments searched the building for clues of a possible arson. With only a few minutes left in the period, we were permitted back into the building. For me, the fire was a mixed blessing. I had dodged 20 minutes of my fourth period class, but with such a motive, I figured I was probably a suspect.

Moments before the lunch bell rang, there was an announcement: "Fourth period will be extended for a few minutes. Keep all students in the rooms." This meant I could not send anyone to the office. Rather than attempt to teach a lesson, I told my students that they could talk quietly as long as they stayed in their seats. Some sport I was. For the entire year students had been out of their seats and screaming while they were instructed to sit silently. Now I was going to "permit" them to whisper?

Keith and Mark started a paper war, throwing wads of paper all over the room. This prompted other students, innocent bystanders, to start screaming. I was trapped with them, so I had to use my only remaining weapon — my voice. I yelled at the class to settle down. "Since you've abused the privilege of talking quietly, there will be no talking for the rest of the time," I shouted. When I turned my head, Mark flicked a paper ball at Karina.

"No throwing paper *or* talking," I screamed, "Just sit there and wait for the bell." My internal clock was signaling my body that it was time for my planning period.

Mark tested me again, knowing he had office immunity. He whispered something to Karina.

"Did you hear what I said?" I shouted. "I want complete silence."

One breath later, he turned around, whispering something to Vinny.

Suddenly, like small animals detecting an oncoming earthquake, everyone became silent and stared at me, waiting. Nostrils flaring, eyes squinting, I stared back at the quiet room. I approached Mark's desk, ready to scream, but fearing I didn't have the energy to do it. If I screamed as intensely as I felt, I would collapse.

I was a failure.

Still, that didn't stop me. I started screaming directly into his eardrum. As my legs buckled, I rested my elbows on his shoulders for support. With my head also resting on his shoulder, I continued to scream as loudly as possible. By the end of my tirade, Mark was basically holding me up as I clutched him, finishing my admonishment. I staggered back to the front of the class and said, "I don't even know what I'll do next." Fortunately, nobody wanted to find out. A minute later a bell sounded to dismiss the class.

Yes, I was a failure.

Assigning blame

*If students are
monsters,
they are only
reluctant
monsters.*

As much as I'd like to blame my first year failures on my
unruly students, I can't and won't. When your house burns
down, who is at fault? Can you put the blame on fire itself,
since that was what most directly caused the destruction?
Or should you blame yourself for falling asleep on the living
room couch while contently smoking a giant cigar? Yes, you
could argue that the fire should have exercised some self-
control, but what court would ever let you sue fire itself for
arson?

Though I'm ignorant of child psychology, I've learned a
lot, first hand, about child "chemistry." Just as a destructive
fire may result from the reaction to circumstances created by
a negligent napper, my students' behavior was a reaction to
my pushover personality. I think the relevant equation is:

$$\text{Students}_{30} + \text{Weak Teacher}_1 \rightarrow \text{Out of Control Classroom}_1$$

If my students were monsters, they were only reluctant
monsters. Think of the character in the movie *An American
Werewolf in London.* He didn't *want* to transform into a
hideous murdering werewolf, but he could not control his
transformation at the sight of the full moon. The students,
in a similar way, were forced against their will to mutate, at
the sight of me, into hideous creatures.

I label them *reluctant* monsters because even with all the
apparent fun they were having, they really hated my class.
They would often scream a final cheer when the period
ended. They often begged to be transferred out. Like most
students, they would much rather have been really learning
in a classroom run by a competent teacher.

The blame for my first year failures lies solely with me. The students were not at all *bad* students. Had I known how to get their attention by starting the year properly and how to keep their attention by really teaching them math, my first year could have been a successful experience for both the students and me. Unfortunately, I did not know how.

In the next few chapters, I will explain how I allowed things to get so out of control, and how — I have since learned — I could have prevented such a fiasco.

When students are out of control, it is probably the teacher's fault.

Being a
REAL Teacher

New teachers need to act like real teachers

Being a REAL Teacher

When people seek the help of a professional, they usually
have certain expectations about how a competent one looks
and behaves.

Recently, I had an appointment with a new dentist.
Entering his office, I was pleased to note several items I had
expected, like a wall of framed diplomas and a pair of color-
ful before-and-after photos of gum disease treatment. He
even had some innovations, including a television mounted
in the ceiling.

I suddenly felt uneasy, however, when I realized that
something vital was missing. He had no spit sink. After I
was seated, I figured that perhaps the sink would rise from
the floor, activated by a remote control, but it never did.
Filling with anxiety, I thought "What's the matter with this
guy? Where am I supposed to spit?" When the time came, I
was appalled as he handed me a small paper cup as his infe-
rior replacement.

Just as adults have their own theories about how "real"
professionals behave, students begin the year with a set of
ideas about what is and what is not a real teacher. They are
disappointed when the professional they so want to trust
does not meet their beliefs about what a "good" one should

*Students don't
necessarily hate
the same old
routine.*

be. (Adults have learned to deal with such disappointment with more maturity than students have. With my disappointing dentist, I didn't, even for a minute, consider torturing him by wedging a small piece of chalk into his blackboard eraser — although I admit I was slightly tempted to switch around his before-and-after gum disease pictures.) A teacher has about one week to prove to the students that he or she is, indeed, a real teacher.

Before my first year of teaching, I was quite aware that students expect their teachers to act a certain way — boring. Anticipating the new school year, their eyes glaze over as they imagine the "typical" teacher with a seating chart, a list of rules and an inevitable, intimidating and immense textbook. Not only are they expecting such a teacher, they are preparing for one the way a football team may prepare for an opponent.

That is why I decided to be different. Before I began my first teaching job, I made the decision to be unlike any teacher students had ever seen before. My class would be a refreshing break from the same old boring routine they had learned to hate.

After the disastrous results, I spent a lot of time thinking about how I could improve. The first conclusion I made was that students don't necessarily hate the same old routine and may not even, in fact, find it boring. In one sense, they *like* teachers to do what they expect them to do, just as I like my dentists to have spit sinks.

I began my path to recovery by accepting the fact that the teacher I *wanted* to be was not the same as the teacher I *had* to be. To endure, I would have to learn how to establish myself as a real teacher in the eyes of my students.

By thinking back to the few times the students from my first year classes had been relatively cooperative, and then remembering exactly what I had been doing at that time, I was able to come up with a list of five rules for real teachers:

1. Real teachers dress the part.
2. Real teachers give a "rules" speech.
3   Real teachers are decisive.
4. Real teachers use textbooks.
5. Real teachers are direct and to the point.

Looking back at my first year of teaching, I realized that I had broken all five of the rules in my very first hour.

A teacher has about a week to prove he or she is a real teacher.

Real teachers dress the part

*Dressing
professionally
is a small but
important
step toward
establishing
respect.*

The first thing my students may have noticed about me
was that, unlike all the other male teachers in the school, I
wasn't wearing a tie. It was a subtle deviation from the norm,
but one I hoped would send an immediate visual message:
"There's a new teacher in town. This guy's going to be different." As I expected, at first sight of me, their faces lit up.
Before class began, I noticed two boys pointing at me and
then exchanging an enthusiastic "high-five." Unfortunately,
their high five didn't indicate respect
for me. It established me, in
their eyes, as someone different — but not, unfortunately,
as a real teacher.

My second year, just to
play it safe, I wore a tie every
day of the school year.

Young teachers
sometimes have trouble
even being recognized
in the halls as teachers.
(One teacher I know got in
trouble her first day for not
having a hall pass.) Dressing
professionally can help distinguish
you from the students themselves — in
their minds *and* in your own.

I can't say that dressing professionally is the most important part of maintaining the respect of one's classes, but I
do know that it can't hurt. It's a small but important step to
take toward establishing respect.

Real teachers give a "rules" speech

As a new teacher, I had decided my first year *not* to review a long list of rules with my classes. Instead of memorizing rules, students could simply figure them out, based on my one guiding principle for class.

"I don't have a list of 20 rules for you," I explained. "All I have is one rule, and it's a rule that I have to follow, too. My rule is, 'Show respect' — respect for me, respect for your classmates and most importantly, respect for yourself.

"All I ask is that before you do something in this class, you ask yourself, 'Will what I'm about to do be disrespectful toward anyone?' If the answer to that question is 'Yes,' or even 'Maybe,' don't do it."

Then a student asked about my pencil sharpening policy. While student teaching, I'd make them laugh with my dry wit so I gave it another shot.

"If you have to sharpen your pencil, raise your hand and ask. But only ask if you really need to sharpen it because here's what I'm going to do. I'm going to take your pencil and poke you with it. If its sharp enough to draw blood, it doesn't really need to be sharpened."

No one laughed. I quickly recanted with, "I'm only kidding."

My second year, the rules speech was a lot less vague — and I didn't try to be cute. Instead of one principle, I distributed a paper with five common, yet practical edicts, like

"Be seated and ready to begin before the tardy bell rings." Students expect real teachers to give them a list of rules. It makes them feel safe.

A list of rules helps students feel safe.

I often hear the suggestion, "Phrase all your rules in the positive. Instead of saying 'Don't talk while others are working,' say, 'Be respectful of others while they are working.'" If you choose to follow this suggestion, I recommend that you don't follow it too rigidly. If the positive rephrasing makes the rule unclear, you should word it in the clear, though not-so-positive, way. If an occasional negative phrasing was good enough for God in the Ten Commandments (It was "Thou shalt not kill," not "Thou shalt permit others to continue living"), then it is good enough for you, too. Clarity is what's important.

Real teachers are decisive

The first day of my first year, unable to shun every boring tradition, I told my classes what supplies I required. "You'll need to have with you each day a pencil and a notebook." A student raised his hand.

"What color does the notebook have to be?"

What kind of fascist teachers were these students accustomed to? I wondered. Still, it was wonderful to see a student interested in pleasing the teacher to that degree. I thought about it for a few seconds.

"Ummmm. Green?" I said. My inflection made it sound more like a question than a directive. Immediately another hand flew up.

"But my mom already bought my supplies, and she didn't know to get green."

"Well, if you already have one, use the one you have. But if you're about to buy one, try to get green. I'm not going to fail you for having a different color."

I've always wondered if that was some kind of trick question, designed to test if I would respond like a real teacher. You can't surprise a real teacher with a question he or she never anticipated since a real teacher has seen it all, many times over. To emulate a real teacher then, you must be prepared to answer questions like the notebook color question confidently, and without hesitation. This doesn't mean you have to spend nights anticipating every potential thing that can be asked. Just be prepared to utter a decisive answer, within two seconds, to just about anything. If you answer fast and decisively, your answer is almost always correct.

*Decisive
answers
inspire
confidence.*

Decisiveness Quiz

Directions: Answer each question with one syllable.

1. Do our notebooks have to be a certain color?

2. Are you sure?

3. What's your first name?

4. Can I go to the bathroom? (with five minutes until the bell)

5. Can I go to the bathroom? (from a girl who is seven months pregnant)

6. Have you ever been high?

7. Can I not turn this in late?

8. Can I (unintelligible gibberish)?

9. Can I not *not* sit in the back?

10. What's the square root of 6241 minus the square root of 5476?

Most of the time the best answer is "No," but be careful in case the question is worded so that the negative response is "Yes." (Compare: "Can we sharpen our pencils without asking?" vs. "Do we have to ask to sharpen our pencils?")

After my first year, I learned how to answer questions like a professional. Occasionally, at the beginning of a class period, a student would ask, "Are we going to the assembly this period?" My usual answer to the surprise assembly question is, "No," though I once accidentally said "Yes." And because I had said "Yes," even though we were supposed to have a test that period, I followed through by ordering everyone to pack up and follow me to the assembly. We weren't even invited to it, but I displayed my teacher confidence at the door and they let us in without hassle.

Now when I say, "No," I say it as if I heard about the assembly weeks ago, carefully weighed the pros and cons, and then slept on it to be sure I considered all the vital factors before settling on my answer. Even a two second pause, or the slightest hint that this is the first I had heard of the assembly, could lead to a student protest.

Teachers should be prepared to utter a decisive answer to any question within two seconds.

I'D SAY "NO" ALTHOUGH ... WELL, I'M NOT SO SURE ... MAYBE ... I'D NEED A WHILE TO THINK ABOUT THAT ... I'LL ASK THE PRINCIPAL THE NEXT TIME I SEE HIM ... OH, WHAT THE HECK, ALL RIGHT ... YES.

Real teachers use textbooks

*I was convinced
that my
homemade
lessons would
work better
than the
textbook.*

Not giving out textbooks on the first day was not an oversight on my part, the first year I taught. "They've had enough of the boring textbooks," I reasoned, "so I'll make my own materials." I told students that, because they were designed especially for them, my lessons would be better than anything they had ever seen in a textbook.

I had reviewed the new sixth grade textbook and found it lacking. (For example, it made an effort to inject multiculturalism by including names from different ethnicities in its examples. However, the examples lacked any context: *Jung Lee wants to know how much carpeting to buy for her trapezoidal-shaped room . . . Maria Garcia wants to know how many inches there are in six feet . . .* Or the token Jewish example, my favorite: *Mark Weinberg makes paperweights in the shape of various three dimensional solids.*)

HALLELUJAH!!
TEXTBOOKS!!

My homemade lessons would be better. As my students eyed the pile of new pink books, I explained that it would be a few weeks before they would receive them. I passed out my own lesson, which included a copy of the times tables. My version, however, had the tables in random order because I wanted students to know them in any order.

"What's this?" Freddy asked.

"It's a special new kind of times table I've invented. It will help you memorize it better."

"Where's seven times three?"

The wacky times tables made students uneasy. A good teacher would have copies of the good times tables.

A few weeks into the year I intercepted a note that read: "This guy don't know how to teach. He don't even give us textbooks, man." When I eventually broke down and distributed the books, the students were so happy that they cheered. Their teacher had finally done something like a real teacher.

Unfortunately, I negated some of the points I had just gained when I refused to complement my action with the standard "Be responsible for this book" lecture. Instead I said something like, "You've heard it a thousand times already so I'm not going to tell you that you need to be responsible for your book. I think you already know that."

While a real teacher passes out the textbooks during the first week, a *good* teacher uses those books soon after they are distributed. Even if you are sure that your homemade activities are superior to anything in the book, you should use the books for a while. That's what good teachers do, at least in the minds of many students. Respect their beliefs about what good teaching entails because they will judge you by their standards.

Teaching from the textbook for a while doesn't mean that you must teach from the textbook forever.

*When they work
out of a text-
book, students
believe they are
learning some-
thing "official."*

Working out of the textbook makes kids feel they are learning something "official." They like to know that they're doing some of the same things as other kids in their grade. Even if you believe the books are deficient, you should find a creative way to work them into your activities in the beginning of the year.

Real teachers are direct and to the point

If you are a real teacher, you learn to say, "Shut up!" — not to your students, of course, but to yourself. My first day I babbled for over half the period about this and that. A mentor of mine once told me, "Teachers have only a certain number of words they can say in the year before their classes tune out. New teachers usually use them up in the first month." By my fourth year, I had learned to take this advice to an extreme, speaking fewer than 100 words to each of my classes on the first day. When the bell sounded, I simply passed out information cards. Instructions on how to fill them out were on the board. As they filled out the card, I passed out the first assignment — a diagnostic quiz. After about 15 minutes, I spoke my first words: "This is the first assignment of the year. Show effort and you'll start the year with an A. I'll decide if you've shown effort by watching you work." Then I shut up and let them continue working.

Teachers have only a certain number of words they can say in the year before their classes tune out.

Being a REAL Teacher

You have to learn the rules before you can break them.

To have control over your classes, you must follow these basic *real* teacher rules. When learning any new skill you often hear the maxim, "You have to learn the rules before you can break them." Even Picasso started by making normal looking paintings.

The good news is that you need to follow the rules only long enough to win students' respect. Once they are convinced you are a real teacher, you can slowly morph into the kind of teacher you've always envisioned yourself to be.

What DOES Work

Mastering a few basics can work wonders

What DOES Work

Not every discipline problem can be prevented. Even a *real* teacher will be tested throughout the year. Luckily, there are methods of classroom management that do work.

Master the teacher look

The "teacher look" is effective because it is mysterious.

Students know that they can't learn from a teacher who isn't in control. The first step in gaining control is mastering "the teacher look."

The teacher look is a visual way for you to get students back on task without disrupting the flow of the class. It is effective for several reasons. First, it addresses any discipline problem without causing a confrontation. When you give a student "the look," she doesn't have to save face since the rest of the class most likely doesn't even know you gave her the look. It is superior to a threat because you haven't committed to doing something you may be unable to follow through on.

The teacher look is also effective because it is mysterious. I've dubbed it the "Rorschach look" because it is interpreted uniquely by each student. One student might view it as, "I know you live with your grandmother and she is fearsome. Do you want me to call her?" Another might interpret it as, "When the volleyball coach hears about this, you'll be running extra laps." And another may think it means, "I'll tell the whole class about that time when you were in first grade and you wet your pants on that field trip to the Museum of Natural History."

The look says, "There's nothing you can do that I haven't already seen, so don't even bother trying." If you haven't mastered it already, I recommend that you practice your teacher look in the mirror. It should be quick and sub-tle — more like a glance. If it's longer than a second or two, it may cause a "What are you looking at?" confrontation.

The teacher look says, "There's nothing you can do that I haven't already seen, so don't even bother trying."

Start with traditional methods

*What matters
is that students
themselves
believe they
have learned.*

Imagine that it is the first week of school. Rather than sub-jecting your classes to a traditional assessment, you develop a complex group activity. You have your rubric, which has been designed to reflect all seven of Howard Gardner's multiple intelligences. You assess students by observing, by asking individuals to explain what they are doing and by evaluating how students contribute to the group. After all, they are learning not only the subject matter but also how to function as a team.

When the activity is over, you are pleased at how well students did. Rather than record grades, you give the stu-dents the option of putting portions of their assignment into their personal portfolios. You are happy that students have mastered the material without resorting to the old-fash-ioned "great equalizer" — a 20 question short answer quiz.

However, if you want them to approach tomorrow's activity with the same positive attitude, students themselves must believe that they did indeed learn. A student is not going to think, "Wow, I like the way this teacher addressed each modality, including the oft-neglected kinesthetic. And I also liked the way alternative assessments were used, which research has shown are more authentic than traditional ones. Open-ended questions, analysis, and synthesis — this activity had it all. It even touched on several higher order thinking skills from Bloom's taxonomy."

For most students, learning is defined as: "Being able to successfully fill out a 20 question worksheet." It doesn't really matter that you may consider such a worksheet a waste of time, especially when they have already proved to you that they have learned. What does matter is that the students believe they have learned.

Start the year with relatively traditional activities and assessments. If students succeed at these, they will label you "good," and you'll soon be able to branch out into more interesting and innovative lessons. Early in the year, this type of thing may seem boring to you, but clear, measurable success is not boring to your students.

At the end of the first week of school, I always give a 20 question quiz. My goal for the first week is to teach my students well enough so that everyone gets a high grade on that first quiz. If they all succeed, they leave my class thinking, "Man, this guy really knows how to teach." Ironically, I convince them that I meet their definition of *good* teacher by betraying my own.

My activities each day of the first week of school are traditional — usually worksheets or questions from their textbook. I work extra hard to grade their assignments thoroughly each night so I can see if anybody is lost. I want to be positive, before they take that first quiz, that everyone is prepared. When I return the graded quizzes on Monday to a class of happy, successful students, I know I have won their respect.

If you can prove to students right away that you are a good teacher, according to their definition, students will be more willing to let you experiment with more inventive teaching strategies that fit your own definition.

*Clear,
measurable
success is
not boring to
students.*

Avoid group work at first

*Put off group
work, at least
until you know
all the students'
names.*

In college, many prospective teachers are advised to use group work as a management tool. The theory is that group work helps prevent the problems associated with student boredom as students work with their peers to more effectively accomplish their goals. But what if their goals are to goof around?

With my first teaching job, I put my students into groups on the fourth day of class. Group work for me quickly came to mean screaming at students in small groups of three to five.

QUIET PLEASE!!
GROUP WORK
IN SESSION!

Group work has its time and place, and many teachers use it quite effectively. But from a discipline point of view, I suggest that you hold off on group work until at least the third or fourth week, and under no circumstances before you know all of the students' names. Putting students into groups right away is like taking your new sports utility vehicle off road the first day you have it. It may be a lot of fun, but it's smarter to get the hang of your new machine first by driving it on safe, paved roads.

It's also important that your students understand that your class is to be taken seriously. Unfortunately, many students perceive working in groups as not really working at all. It's better to set a serious tone before you allow students to work in groups.

Many students perceive working in groups as not really working at all.

Avoid confrontation

Needless confrontation can turn small problems into huge power struggles.

When you confront a student in front of the class, you can turn a small discipline problem into a huge power struggle between you and the student. This consumes quite a bit of time and energy.

If two kids are chatting too loudly, rather than say something, I may just give them the "Shhh" signal with my index finger in front of my lips. If I'm in the middle of a lesson, I may just walk over to one of their desks, while I continue to teach, giving it a few subtle taps.

Avoid confrontation, if possible, even when you are changing a student's assigned seat. Do it before class even begins, if possible. If you must do it in the middle of class, simply walk over and say, "I want you to sit in that seat over there." If you then stand there and wait for the student to move, he never will. In order to get him to move, you must walk away and continue teaching. Look a few minutes later, and the student will almost always be in the new seat.

Always speak as though you expect students to do what you ask, and allow them room to do it.

Make surprise calls to parents

While threatening to call parents is not an effective technique for teachers, actually calling them can sometimes be very effective. My first rule of calling parents is that it must be done without warning. This method requires patience. Wanting immediate results, it is tempting to say, "I'll be calling home tonight." But for all the reasons I outlined earlier, you must resist this urge. It is impossible to guarantee that you will make contact with the parents. If you call without warning, the student will never know that you tried and failed.

One of the best parts about the surprise parent call is when the student comes to class the next day and gives you a few minutes of free advertising: "Man, Teacher called my parents last night." Even if students act tough and pretend they don't care that you called, all the other kids in class get the message that you are a teacher of action — not words. I've taught in three schools, none of which had what I would call active parental support, yet no student I've ever encountered really wanted to have a teacher call his parents.

My second rule about parent phone calls is to keep them direct and short. Teachers are often advised to start each parent conference with something positive, or to phrase what the student did wrong in a positive way. For instance, instead of saying, "Your child is jumping around all the time," say "Your child has a lot of energy."

I disagree with this advice. While I try to say at least one positive thing during the conversation, I don't do it right at the beginning. "Your son did really well on a quiz last week" is not the best topic sentence for a discussion on how

Calling parents without warning is far more effective than warning students that you will call.

Don't waste your time tying to get cooperation from parents who aren't cooperative.

he was shooting rubber bands across the room this week. Parents also appreciate it when you don't waste their time with indirect euphemisms they have to struggle to decipher. A nice side effect of being direct is that your parent calls will last under five minutes.

Though a vast majority of parents are cooperative, there are a few who are difficult. They think their child is perfect and won't believe you when you say that she did something wrong. Don't waste your time with this type of parent. If you don't accomplish anything in your five minute time limit, just end the call and try to avoid contact with that parent in the future.

Ignore selectively

Some classroom problems are simply not worth expending the energy it would take to deal with them. Sometimes the most effective tactic is to ignore what happened. For example, suppose you tell a student to put away her magazine. Although she complies, she mutters something profane about you under her breath.

Though teachers pride themselves on having developed bionic hearing (the phrase "I heard that" is a common part of many teachers' vocabularies), sometimes it is better to conceal such super-human powers. If your students think that you didn't hear it, they will not think that you let her get away with saying it. At worst, they will think you are a little hard of hearing.

To successfully pull off the ignoring trick, you have to be prepared to suppress your reflex to react immediately to

Suppress your reflex to react immediately to every little thing.

every little thing. You need to give yourself an extra half second between the time something happens and the time you react, so that you can decide if this is something you should choose to ignore.

"How much," you may ask, "can be reasonably ignored?" Surprisingly, a lot. Even experienced teachers occasionally have a bad day. You know the kind: Nothing is going right. The kids aren't into it, and neither are you. No particular student or group of kids is at fault. It's just one of those days.

When a day like this occurs, you have only two options when you greet the class the following day. One is the "What happened yesterday is not acceptable" speech. This, I believe, can only worsen things. It indicates that the teacher is in panic mode over something that the kids most likely have already forgotten. The other option is to ignore it. Yes, as much as a whole day can be ignored when there is no better option.

Another useful tactic that violates the idea of the omnipotent teacher is to pretend sometimes that you are oblivious. If two students are talking instead of working on an assignment, I like to bring them more work and say, with a straight face, "That's great that you guys are finished already. Here, you can start working on the next assignment so you're not bored."

Pretend sometimes that you are oblivious.

Seek advice

If you want my advice — which you probably don't, either because you're a first year teacher who thinks you know it all, or because you're a second year teacher who knows you do, or because you're a third or fourth year teacher who knows that although you don't know it all, neither do I — here it is, anyway: All advice is good, even when it is bad.

All advice is good, even when it is bad.

While traveling cross country to Los Angeles in 1991 for my first teacher training classes, I spoke with a drunk plumber at a tavern in Wyoming. When he heard that I was becoming a teacher, he offered this piece of teaching advice: "On the first day of school, find the biggest kid in the class and watch him. The second his mouth opens, Wham! Grab him by the lapels. Get him down on the ground, and put your knee into his chest. You won't have any problems for the rest of the year."

I decided to ignore his suggestion. My goal was not to intimidate, but to motivate. Still, his words were difficult to forget. My first day teaching, I noticed that there was one kid who was obviously the largest. I couldn't help but watch that proportionately large mouth, and when it opened, as the plumber predicted it would, I realized I was in trouble. She wasn't wearing lapels.

My failure to act on my first discipline problem resulted in growing chaos, which in turn caused me great digestive problems. I spent many of my first semester's planning periods in the faculty men's room. It was there that I often encountered a lazy teachers' aide named Mr. Travis. When I told him about my troubles, he advised me on curriculum.

*Learn to find
the truth in any
advice.*

"Make them write. They like that. Give them some pages from the textbook and have them copy."

I dismissed this idea immediately. My teaching philosophy did not include mindless busy work. My first unit for my sixth grade math classes centered on higher thinking skills in multiplication. They would draw pictures of multiplication word problems. They would write stories about multiplication word problems. They would play a multiplication game that I invented (Roll two dice. If the sum of the numbers is even, move right. If it is odd, move left. Multiply the two numbers together. If there is another way to represent that product with two different factors, pick a card.) In doing so, I took the one thing the students felt they understood — multiplication — and showed that even that was too complicated for them. Not only did I fail to keep it simple, I made students uneasy about math.

Once students realized they weren't learning, they stopped cooperating. Two months into the school year, a girl named Ivette refused to even open her books. Frustrated, I approached her desk, slammed my hand down on top of her books and swept them off her desk and into the wall 12 feet away. Enraged, she stood up and hit me. The stress from this incident caused my internal blender to shift from "mince" to "puree." After class that day, I sprinted to the restroom, where I related the story to Mr. Travis. He said, "They hit me all the time. It's no big deal. Just ignore it."

I couldn't ignore her action. All my students had heard about it, and I knew that if there were no consequences, I could expect a very difficult year. But since I provoked her by acting unprofessionally, my principal had to rule in favor of the student at the expulsion hearing.

After that, there was no way to salvage my reputation.

By the end of my first year, I realized that my mistake
was not that I didn't accept advice. My mistake was that I
didn't know how to accept advice. All advice, whether it
sounds good or bad, has merit. People share advice because
it has worked for them. New teachers should at least listen
to the advice, analyze it and try to figure out how to make it
work for them.

In reacting to incorrect student responses in class, I have
learned to find something salvageable in even the most dubi-
ous comment. It's important to find something "right" about
any answer so I don't discourage future participation. This
ability to listen to the world through rose colored hearing
aids has also helped me listen to advice from others in a new
way.

"Grab him by the lapels"? By this, I think the plumber
really meant, "Be decisive. Actions are more powerful than
threats. Let them know that you're in charge. Be confident."
It's some of the best advice I have ever heard.

"Make them write"? In three words, the teachers' aide
corrected one of the most common mistakes of new teachers
— making things too complicated. I now interpret the man's
advice to mean "Keep it simple at first. Do something safe."
When students are allowed to experience success, they feel
confidence in themselves and in their teacher. Then you can
attempt more innovative and complicated activities.

"Just ignore it"? Mr. Travis' advice was the perfect complement to "Grab him by the lapels," even if he didn't apply
his advice to the proper circumstances. I believe he meant
that silence can be, at times, the most powerful action.
Perhaps what he meant to say was, "Don't fight every battle.
Choose only the ones you're sure you can win. And of
those, only enter conflicts that you can win without expend-

*Actions are
more powerful
than threats.*

*Silence can be,
at times, the
most powerful
action.*

ing too much energy." Though this was not an example of something worth ignoring for me, there were other times throughout the year that I could have taken this advice.

One last thing: Don't try to apply my advice about advice to my advice itself. My advice only applies to everyone else's advice. Advice from me, of course, should be taken word for word!

FINDING THE GOOD IN ANY ANSWER

Test your ideas critically

For new teachers, too much optimism can be dangerous. As a new teacher, I found great satisfaction in mentally listing all the reasons why a lesson plan idea was so perfect. By the time I realized that it had flaws, I would already be using it in the classroom. The problems with the lesson would often exacerbate my discipline difficulties.

To avoid this common experience, teachers need to think one step deeper while planning. We expect our students to think critically about what they do, yet, ironically, we sometimes fail to be critical thinkers ourselves.

In addition to listing all the things that are good about an idea, you should also list the things that could be *bad* about the idea. Before sending your lessons into combat, give them the equivalent of a military inspection. (No, I was never in the military. If given the choice between boot camp and reliving my first year, however, I would choose boot camp without hesitation.)

When this process is finished, one of three things can happen: (1) You will decide to do the lesson exactly as originally planned, (2) You will scrap the lesson entirely, or (3) You will fix the lesson up, retaining its good qualities, while eliminating some of its potential flaws.

An example. Suppose that your lesson idea is "an empowering alternative to the rules speech the first day of school." Instead of just telling the students the rules, you want to make an activity out of it. You want them to brainstorm what the rules should be.

You first think of all the positive features of this idea:

Give your lessons the equivalent of a military inspection before sending them into combat.

1. Kids are less likely to break rules that they created.
2. When kids break the rules, you can say, "You're breaking your own rule," and they will stop.
3. Kids often make up even tougher rules than you would have given them.
4. By letting the kids make up the rules, they will feel like they have some power and will not need to prove they have power by breaking the teacher's rules.

*Optimism
should not
prevent you
from seeing the
flaws in a lesson
plan.*

It is easy to think of reasons why this lesson is a great idea. What you should do is go on and create a list of what is *bad* about the idea. To approach this part of the task objectively, just remember: Don't be afraid to find fault in the idea. Just because the idea isn't perfect doesn't mean that you have to scrap it. The bad list may help you to modify the idea so that it will be more successful.

Here are some negative features of the make-the-rules activity:

1. Kids may make up easy rules, forcing you to say, "Come on. Is that really a rule that will promote learning in this class?"
2. Kids may see it as a trick that's intended to make them feel like they have some say in the class, when in reality they know that the final rules will be the ones the teacher wants.
3. Kids may start arguing with each other about the rules, and a fight may break out (assuming, that is, that they didn't already establish a no fighting rule).
4. Kids may make the rules harder than you wanted to make them, leaving you in the awkward position of having to enforce rules you don't want. For example, maybe they will decide that nobody can ever go to the

restroom, while you would prefer that they have that right.

5. Kids are already going to try to get as much power as possible. Why give them a head start by telling them, directly, that they set the rules?

Now it is up to you to decide which list is more compelling. I believe, in this example, that the negatives outweigh the positives. Though I do know some teachers who have used this activity successfully, they were teachers who already had strong reputations. This idea may be one worth storing away until you have established yourself as a good classroom manager.

Remember that this exercise works for both lesson ideas and for discipline management strategies. Get in the habit of thinking more critically, in both senses of the word, and your classroom will run more smoothly.

Flawed lessons can exacerbate discipline problems in the classroom.

A LESSON GONE WRONG

Developing a Teacher Persona

Find a style that fits your personality

Developing a Teacher Persona

As a teacher, which movie character would you most like to emulate?

A. Robin Williams in *Dead Poets Society*
B. Michelle Pfeiffer in *Dangerous Minds*
C. Edward James Olmos in *Stand and Deliver*
D. Arnold Schwarzenegger in *Kindergarten Cop*
E. Arnold Schwarzenegger in *The Terminator*

The differences between movie teaching and real teaching

Movie teaching

The first day is hard; the rest of the year is easy.

As a secondary teacher, you have one class of 15 students.

You give students candy to motivate them and get their attention.

You struggle with incompetent administrators.

Sometimes you feel like the only competent teacher in the school.

When you resign, you pack all your stuff into one file box.

Real teaching

The first day is easy; the rest of the year is hard.

As a secondary teacher, you have five or six classes of 30–40 students.

You give students candy and they become hyper and throw the wrappers on the floor for you to pick up after class.

You struggle with incompetent administrators.

Sometimes you feel completely incompetent.

When you resign, you need a truck for all your accumulated junk.

Movie teaching	Real teaching
There's one smart pregnant girl in your classes.	There are at least two or three smart pregnant girls in your classes.
A bright boy quits the gang to dedicate himself to school.	A bright boy quits school to dedicate himself to the gang.
At the end of the year, students rally around you begging you not to quit.	At the end of the year, students rally around you begging for make-up work so they won't have to go to summer school.

Though there are many effective teacher personas, finding the one that best works for you is not simply a matter of choosing from a list. As with clothing styles, not every teaching style looks good on every person. A common suggestion, then, is to not have a style but to just be yourself.

But what is "yourself"? For me, it has several definitions. (No, I haven't been diagnosed with multiple personalities. Many people who know me would argue that I barely have even *one*.) "Myself" with my family is different than "myself" with my friends. And even if I could accurately define "myself," who is to say that this self would also be my ideal teacher self?

Developing a Teacher Persona

When I exaggerated, the students instantly knew I was bluffing.

I have struggled since 1981, when I won my junior high school's "number sense" math competition, to overcome the stigma of being labeled a nerd. In high school, I quit participating in math competitions. I locked away some of the nerdiest parts of myself in an attempt to be accepted socially by the "in" crowd. Though I listened to the cool music and sneaked into the cool parties, it didn't matter because everyone already knew my history.

When I went away to college, I thought to myself, "Nobody knows me here. I have no past. Finally, I can be anyone I want." Given an opportunity for a fresh start with new people, I decided I would reinvent myself and become the cool person I always knew I could be.

Though my plan didn't work in college, I still found myself having similar thoughts as I began my teaching career. "I have no past. I can be anyone I want. I can be cool."

I failed during the first week. A student asked if I had ever taught before. Exaggerating my recent student teaching experience, I said, "Well, I taught for a while in Los Angeles. The kids thought they were tough, but they really weren't."

The students instantly knew I was bluffing.

After suffering through my first year, I knew I would have to try something different for my second year. I was transferred to a high school where I was, once again, unknown and ready for a new beginning.

I knew that "cool" didn't work for me. Nor could I be my nerdy self for fear that these high school students would make fun of me, just as high school students had when I was a student. I was concerned because I didn't know what identity to assume.

For the first week of school that year, I displayed a neutral personality, concentrating solely on my teaching. The first day, while my natural inclination was to tell them a little about myself, I just did what I had seen in movies. I picked up a stick of chalk and wrote my name on the board. "My name is Mr. Rubinstein, and this is Algebra II. Does anyone have something different on their schedule?" I hadn't realized that their schedules were printed before I was hired, so my name wasn't on any of them.

*I decided to
try starting out
with a neutral
personality.*

A girl raised her hand and said, "My schedule says my teacher's name is 'Vacancy.'" Though this was, perhaps, an opportunity for me to demonstrate my sense of humor with a flippant comment like, "That's me. My name used to be Vacancy, but I had it legally changed," I resisted. I wasn't sure that *funny* was my optimum teacher persona. It was too early to tell, so I just said, "Cross it out and write in Rubinstein — that's R-U-B-I-N-S-T-E-I-N," and passed out the first assignment.

In the middle of the second week, however, I got my first clue about which direction to take with my identity. Going over a word problem on the board, I had to multiply 52 by 16. Having won the "number sense" competition in junior high, I knew a shortcut for multiplying by 16, since it is a power of 2. After only two seconds of thought, I wrote down the answer: 832. I noticed several students looking at each other and smiling. They were impressed that I could calculate in my head.

Developing a Teacher Persona

*Not every
teaching style
looks good on
every teacher.*

I was stunned. For 12 years I had tried to cover up my nerdiness, only to find some students actually looking impressed by something nerdy I had done. I saw then that I wouldn't have to struggle to pretend to be someone else after all. All I would do is unleash the geek inside me that was screaming to emerge. I decided to permit my repressed nerd to go wild.

The nerdier I became, the more my students responded. I would even go home and practice intellectual feats to enhance my image. While teaching a ninth grade class about circles, I mentioned *pi*. "Most people think that pi is equal to 3.14," I said, "but really it goes on. It starts out 3.141592653589793238462 . . ." I continued on for the first 100 digits.

When students asked how I was able to memorize that many numbers, I just told them, "Well, I don't have to memorize any phone numbers since I don't have any friends. Fourteen phone numbers would already be 98 digits."

Since I often had about 20 pens in my shirt pockets, two of my students bought me a gift of a white plastic pocket protector. Proudly, I wore it for the rest of the year. I got a kick out of the fact that while my students thought I was the biggest nerd that ever lived, I knew that I was really only an above average nerd, an above average nerd who was — they would have been shocked to know — dating one of their teachers.

Don't smile until Christmas. For another aspect of my teacher identity, I adopted the old teacher slogan, "Don't smile until Christmas break." (The year before I hadn't followed that maxim; consequently, Christmas break was the next time I *felt* like smiling.) My goal was not really to refrain from smiling, but to refrain from yelling. I didn't believe it was possible to limit only one side of my emotional spectrum, so the only solution was a completely shut down at the source. My emotions were connected to an on/off switch, not a dimmer.

The class rules for my second year were excessive: No socializing. No smiling. No laughing. No using the restroom. No sneezing. These rules were not posted in the back of the room; they were posted in the back of my mind. The rules were not for my students. They were for me.

I practiced my facial expressions in the mirror the night before school began. Relaxed position was eyes squinted, mouth in a tightish pout. For disappointment, my eyes would squint a little tighter. For approval, I would relax my eyes slightly and nod my head slowly. When something funny happened, I had a method of suppressing smiles. By biting the inside of my cheek, I prevented the smile on two fronts: My teeth would physically hold down the corners of my mouth. Also, the pain countered some of my desire to smile.

I had similar techniques for other involuntary actions, like early-morning yawns and pollen-induced sneezes. Any of these actions would have revealed that I was partially human and therefore susceptible to human weaknesses. The consequences of a negligent lapse could be devastating, I believed. If someone were to say, "Need a tissue to blow your nose, Mr. Rubinsneeze?" all would be over. I felt as if I were one of those Buckingham Palace guards, with my students — like American tourists — trying to make me react.

Finding an effective teacher persona may take some experimentation.

*Allow yourself
room to change
directions if a
style doesn't
work for you.*

Sophomore Sarina Holmes was my sixth period class clown. To introduce the study of geometric formulas in her class, I offered some historical context.

"Today we're going to learn about circles. Now people have been interested in circles for thousands of years. Why? What's the most famous circle of all? Yes, Sarina?"

"Pancakes."

Sarina was the first student to perfect an imitation of me. She loved to quote what I once said to a gum-cracking student: "Notice: I'm also chewing gum, but I'm not making any noise." She also mocked my internal clock: "Don't pack up yet. We still have three minutes and eighteen seconds, enough time for 12 more problems."

One Friday in September, my sixth-period class finished early. I told students, "By working hard, you've earned some free time. Relax for the remaining two minutes and 15 seconds. You can talk to each other until the bell rings."

"Mr. Rubinstein," Kendra called out, "how old are you?"

"Do you have a girlfriend?" Sarina followed.

"I said you should talk to each other, not to me."

So they talked to each other *about* me. "He never gets mad," Kendra commented.

"Yeah," Sarina said, "when he gets mad, he probably just goes, 'Notice: I'm mad, but I'm not showing it.'" Her exaggerated nasal impression of me, combined with the not-so-exaggerated truth of what she said penetrated my armor. Biting my cheek wasn't enough. I had to turn my back to the room and compose myself. When Sarina was leaving she said, "You smiled." I looked back at her and responded, "That must have been someone else."

Sarina, like everyone else, eventually abandoned the futile quest to make me smile. It was like trying to insult

an ATM machine or argue with a parking meter. You can't
ruffle the feathers of a mechanical chicken.

I would never have discovered this effective teacher persona for myself if I had predetermined the kind of teacher
I would be. The trick to finding your ideal teacher persona
is to start neutral and then experiment a little with some
different styles. Can you be "Funny Teacher"? Make a joke,
and see if they laugh. See also how they behave after the
joke. Ask a student about his home life, and you may discover, from his trusting response, that you've got "Counselor
Teacher" potential.

Think of yourself as a soccer goalie waiting for a penalty
kick, not leaning too far one way or the other, ready and
in position to change directions if necessary. Don't commit
to one persona or another until you feel confident that you
have found the one that will work for you.

*Don't
predetermine
the kind of
teacher you
will become.*

The dangers of not being yourself

*I had become
Dr. Jekyll and
Mr. Rubinstein.*

It is true that being a super nerd was easy for me in many ways, since it was just a magnified trait of my true personality. However, being an emotionless robot was very taxing. In real life I loved to laugh and smile.

Well past the honeymoon period, before Thanksgiving break, I decided I would lighten up slightly. Defrosting myself would be a dangerous and delicate process, so I carefully heeded the warning on my Thanksgiving turkey: "If you rush the defrosting process, you can destroy the turkey. The outside will rot while the core remains ice." I decided to wait for appropriate thawing opportunities, which were happening often.

I had trouble taking advantage of them. Two students, Damon and Sarina, would come after school daily to chat, but I maintained my mask, even under such safe conditions. They would start telling me funny stories about what they did over the weekend, and though I was tempted to chime in with some stories of my own, I merely nodded contentedly.

In class one day a student named Beatrice asked me if I was married. Not knowing what to answer, I bluntly responded, "I don't know."

I found that I had created a demon — Mr. Rubinstein's monster. I had become Dr. Jekyll and Mr. Rubinstein. My act was no longer an act. I was finding it nearly impossible to discard the emotionless Mr. Rubinstein.

Yet, despite my impersonal approach, the students actually liked the way I taught. I reasoned, "It's better to be a teacher who can't be human than a human who can't teach."

Everything changes. On the day we returned to school after Thanksgiving break, my first period class was in a strange mood. They were whispering a lot instead of paying attention to my lesson on compound inequalities. Making sure they hadn't forgotten who was in charge, I came down hard on them with a series of deadly teacher looks. The next period, when the morning announcements were read, I learned why they were distracted.

"Attention students . . ."

Throughout the day classes were always being interrupted by meaningless chatter. I sighed.

" . . . a terrible tragedy . . ."

Was the principal intending to threaten the entire school, again, in response to the recent graffiti epidemic?

" . . . Nohemi Treveño was an honor student. We will all miss her greatly."

A girl had died? To my relief, I didn't recognize the name. I had a Nohemi, but not a Nohemi Treveño.

" . . . Excuse me, I'm sorry. Her name was Nohemi Torres."

And that's how I learned of the loss of my student. Nohemi Torres was 16 years old. She had been shot in the head by her ex-boyfriend.

Two weeks earlier, she had asked me to write her a recommendation for National Honor Society. Knowing it was a formality, I quickly filled the small space provided: "Nohemi is a diligent worker and an excellent person. Her dedication to her work, and to after school PSAT preparation, is unmatched." But I left out her most special qualities. Attentive and interested, serious but happy, she justified my decision to teach.

Nohemi's last words to me were, "Thank you."

103

*I felt like crying,
but I had
forgotten how.*

Nohemi's last words to me were, "Thank you," after I gave her back the recommendation form. I don't remember my last words to her. I know they weren't "You're very welcome. Congratulations. You earned it." Most likely, I grunted something like "Mmm hmmm" in my trademark monotone with my expressionless mouth.

Two hours before the announcement, I had casually marked Nohemi absent in my first period class. The students were not surprised at my lack of reaction, even though they must have assumed I already knew Nohemi had been killed. When I heard the announcement, I felt like crying, but I didn't. I had forgotten how.

The next day, I addressed her classmates and her empty desk: "I wish I knew how to teach you to deal with this. Actually, I need someone to teach me. Maybe you're thinking, 'What good is going to school and learning algebra if I could be dead tomorrow?' I don't think Nohemi would have said that. She's probably up in heaven now, and as great as it is there, she's probably wishing she could be right here, in this desk. She loved school. Nohemi is dead, but her dreams are still right here. You know what they were: To learn. To

have a successful future. She knew that to fulfill those dreams would take courage and effort. Now it's all of you who need that courage and effort. Now it is your responsibility to adopt those dreams and keep them alive."

I'll always regret that the classroom persona I thought I needed interfered with my desire to let my students know that I cared. I never looked at Nohemi and said sincerely, "I'm really proud of you." Instead I wrote about how "diligent" she was and how her work was "unmatched." If Nohemi knew how fond I was of her, she knew in spite of my efforts to hide it. She was perceptive enough to do that.

I'm almost positive.

I never understood why the counselors didn't come to my first period class that day to tell us what had happened. I also wondered why none of my students told me, either. One possibility is that they assumed I already knew and that I was a heartless person for making them be quiet. The other possibility is that they just didn't feel comfortable enough to tell me.

Either way, I saw that something was seriously wrong. It was time to make more serious efforts to lighten up.

Slow progress. Although I made attempts to become more human, the process was very slow. I was reluctant to let go. It wasn't until the end of the school year, at the Cinco de Mayo festival, that I finally completed my human transformation.

I remained stoic and in character for the entire morning, even as a marching mariachi band, complete with dancers, patrolled the halls. After third period, the entire school would congregate for the annual carnival and food court.

Though less than a month remained in the school year, I felt I couldn't risk revealing my human side. A slip could not only destroy the last few weeks of school but could possibly corrupt the next year as well. While the other teachers wore T-shirts and shorts in preparation for the festival's main attraction, the dunking booth, I wore my normal

My progress towards becoming more human was slow.

clothes for classes, stashing a set of casual clothes in the
trunk of my car for later.

The dunking booth was a primitive mechanical marvel.
The eight-foot plank was held down by a lever that was connected to the saucer-sized circular target. The water in the
tub, a large unpainted aluminum reservoir, jiggled below.

Mr. Berra volunteered first. As the favorite teacher of
most seniors, he handled the dunking booth the way he
handled his class — loudly.

"Hey, Robert, give it a shot. You were on the baseball
team. Oh yeah, I forgot, you never left the bench.

"Mario, try to dunk me, or are you worried that your
girlfriend there will think you're a wuss when you can't even
reach me?

"Marisol, just pretend that the target is Mario's ex-girl-
friend."

Taunting the crowd further, Berra lay down on his side,
like a bathing suit model. He supported his head with one
hand and covered a dramatic yawn with the other. After five
minutes of missed attempts, Sarina, class clown, rushed the
target and pushed it, plopping an unsuspecting Berra into
the tank. After Mr. Berra, a full list of teachers and administrators was scheduled, including the principal and Mrs.
Sommers, the "sexy" teacher.

Now in blue jeans, a black T-shirt, sneakers and sunglasses,
I conspicuously traversed the transformed courtyard, parting
a sea of gawking students. Heads turned, followed by hysterical student laughter. Some laughed because, for the first
time, I looked "cool." Others laughed because, once again, I
didn't. Tejano music blared over the P.A. system, while students twisted to the lambada and merengue. A few dancing

*I conspicuously
traversed the
courtyard,
parting a sea
of gawking
students.*

students signaled an invitation for me to join them, but I ignored them.

The "no water gun" rule was temporarily suspended. Everyone avoided squirting me, however. I wasn't the kind of person you did that to. My robotic circuits might short.

The commotion at the dunking booth, I assumed, was a result of Mrs. Sommers wearing less than usual. When I arrived, I discovered that Sommers was not in the booth. Nobody was. I eyed the vacant seat. The crowd chanted, "Rub-in-stein, Rub-in-stein!" As I edged closer to the tank, the screams intensified.

I slowly ascended the ladder. My feet dangling from the plank, I strategically summoned Sarina to guard the target. Mostly, she would be protecting me from herself. With Sarina at her post, I knew nobody else would push the target. (Class clown etiquette dictates that no one should ever take on the clown's role, especially when she's watching.)

For two dollars, some kid I had never even seen before purchased eight opportunities to dunk me. All missed. Others took turns. Everyone missed. Students probably wondered if, when I hit the water, I would melt like the Wicked Witch of the West.

Finally, Sarina abandoned her post and waved a dollar at the booth supervisor. She walked to the line while the other students cheered. In her nasal impersonation of me, she said, "According to my calculations, the ball must be thrown at a velocity of 35 miles per hour at an angle of elevation of 18 degrees." The crowd howled. She then stood at the line, shook off a few signals from the invisible catcher and chewed some invisible tobacco. Borrowing from either Pete Townsend or a Bugs Bunny cartoon, she swung her arm sev-

*The crowd
chanted,
"Rub-in-stein,
Rub-in-stein!"*

eral times, refusing to release the ball. Then she stopped and shook off another signal. "Throw it," someone screamed.

She lobbed the ball into the air, and while we all watched its graceful arc, someone charged the tank. There was a moment between the instant I began to fall and the instant I realized I was falling. And in that moment, for the first time all year, I was completely unguarded.

Students danced around me, pointing.

Emerging from the tank, I still didn't smile — not because I was masking my emotions, but because I was cold and covered with unsanitary water. I could hide it when I was happy. I could hide it when I was angry. I could not hide the fact that I was drenched.

As I climbed from the tank and headed for my towel, students danced around me, pointing. Maybe they were happy because I hadn't melted.

Maybe they were happy because I had.

Avoiding certain personas

You should feel free to experiment with a number of different teacher personas that are similar to your own. However, there are some personalities you should avoid.

*The dean
said, "Don't
patronize these
students, or
they'll eat you
for lunch."*

The martyr. "Saving the children" was one of the main reasons I applied to Teach For America and became a teacher. For the TFA application, I had to answer this essay question: "Based on your own experiences, what do you have to offer children from an inner city and/or rural background in terms of their own (a) educational development, (b) motivation and (c) self-esteem"?

I get nauseous when I now reread sections of my answer. "When a student sees someone like me — a person who appears to have sacrificed much in order to teach, it is possible for me to gain his/her respect as one who has broken the stereotype." Later in the essay I wrote, "I am not the enemy of the poor, and neither are millions of others who dedicate themselves to helping the culturally-less fortunate. I offer myself as a stepping stone to help many needy youngsters into a world of opportunity. The beauty of this metaphorical scene is that everyone including me, the stone, will be happy if I am successful."

Before my first day of teaching, Armando Alaniz, my dean of instruction, pulled my friend Jon Fish and me into his office. "Let's get one thing straight.

*A teacher's goal
should not be to
"save" students
but to teach
them.*

You're not here to save these students. You're here to teach them, and if teaching them happens to save them, then great. But don't you patronize these students because if you do they'll eat you for lunch." This short, yet powerful speech put a new perspective on what I was about to do. Had it not been for Armando Alaniz, now a high school principal, my students would have had one more reason to make my life miserable.

The just-one-of-them teacher. I often hear new teachers say things like, "I can relate to these students because I was just like them when I was in school." I advise these teachers to be careful. First, if you succeed at convincing your students you are one of them, you may lose their respect. Also, as I have learned, if you fail at your attempt to fit in, the results can be devastating.

My first job was in a poor school, and I was concerned that my students would resent what they might perceive as their rich-boy teacher. To prepare for the job, I went with my mother to Macy's for some inexpensive, modest clothing: three pairs of khaki pants, five striped, short-sleeved dress shirts, five ties and one pair of brown leather boat shoes.

According to district statistics, my school was "poor." Perhaps my students hadn't read the statistics. Wearing the latest designer clothes and accessories, they competed in a daily fashion show. On their feet they sported the newest model Air Jordans, which cost easily over $100. They wore expensive jeans and expensive Starter jackets. Many enjoyed these small luxuries at the expense of certain necessities, like phone service.

By November, my own shoes revealed some abuse. The soles were falling off, while my sock peeped through an

expanding hole over the left big toe. In my sixth period
class, an observant Jorge "Smiley" Reyes, called out, "Why
don't you get new shoes?"

I recalled one of my former teachers from Long Island.
In a class populated by the children of white-collar professionals, Mr. Auletta would entertain the class with jokes
about his poverty, as an underpaid teacher. Since, as a student, I had enjoyed this self-deprecating humor, I tried to
utilize it as a teacher. To Smiley's question, I responded, "I
can't buy new shoes because I'm poor."

On a budget, for the first time in my life, I *felt* poor.
Graduating from an expensive college, I expected to have
money right away. But as they say, "You get out of college
what you put into it," which I did: $21,000 a year. Still, I
kind of liked the novelty of being poor. Clipping coupons
and eating pasta most nights was fun, like a game. Plus, it
gave me the right to complain about being broke, as my students often did.

For example, Sergio complained when I told my classes
to buy rulers, which would cost about 75 cents at most
drug stores. Sergio said, "I can't afford that. I'm just a poor
Mexican." When I told him I would lend him a ruler, he
said, "That's OK. I'll buy one. Do you know if the drug
stores take food stamps?" Everyone laughed.

For me, another "fun" part about being poor was developing hatred for the rich. At the supermarket, I would scoff
at the spoiled snots ordering their parents to purchase the
latest designer breakfast cereal. At teacher conventions, I
would meet educators from the wealthier suburbs. While
they spoke of their innovative lessons, I could only think
of the bashing sessions in the faculty lounge at my school,

*If you succeed
at convincing
students you are
one of them,
you may lose
their respect.*

*My lie was an
obvious attempt
to manipulate
students.*

where my colleagues would remark about the suburban
teachers, "Sure, anyone can teach *those* students."

My "because I'm poor," response to Smiley's shoe inqui-
ry did not get the reaction I expected. A few students gave
me skeptical looks while Angela shouted, "No you're not.
You're rich!"

"Why do you say that?"

"Your glasses. We were in the glasses store the other day,
and those cost $200."

The class glared at my glasses.

"My dad bought these for me when I was in college.
He's got money, but he stopped buying me stuff when I
started working."

Not good enough. Being rich is genetic.

My glasses, which were supposed to help me see more
clearly, helped me be seen more clearly. Even the students
who had not yet mastered the times tables had the induc-
tive powers to understand that I could never again be fully
trusted — typical of a spoiled rich kid with his fancy glasses.

My lie was insulting because it was an obvious attempt
to manipulate the students into believing we were in the
same boat. "I'm poor," was like saying, "We're poor." Most
of all, though, they resented this lie because with my state-
ment, I so easily accomplished something they had only
dreamed of. I lied about being poor.

Instead of trying to fit in with my students, I eventually
learned to use my differences as a way to entertain my classes. Sometimes, just to drive home the point that I was not
one of them, I would give my own interpretation of favorite
student expressions. When a female student answered a

Teacher persona cut-out doll

question correctly, for example, I might say, "You go girl!" in my most nerdy voice.

The hero teacher. For some people, it is not good enough to be known as a good teacher, or even as the best teacher. They need to be known as the *only* capable teacher in the school. A teacher like this often amasses a loyal following of students who have been brainwashed to think this teacher is the only one they can learn from. I realized that I was in danger of becoming one of these teachers, my second year, when some of my students began coming to my room after school to whine and complain about some of my colleagues.

At first I listened, grateful that the complaints were *to* me rather than *about* me. I didn't understand the potential harm of this practice until I witnessed another teacher's after-school counseling sessions.

Carl Lowrey had a following of former students who would visit his room each day after school for extra math tutoring. Some teachers referred to this group as "The Lowrey Babies." In his room, they would find an overly receptive listener.

"I wish I still had you for math. I got Mr. Aaron."

"Well, he's new," he explained. "Bring your notes to me after school, and I'll show you how to do it." Sometimes after they complained enough to him, Mr. Lowrey would ask the counselors to switch students into his class.

Or he would savor the complaints, encouraging the students to elaborate. He seemed to get a thrill from them, hearing insults of others as praise for himself.

"Mrs. Parks doesn't teach."

"Doesn't teach? What does she do then?"

Some teachers need to be known as the ONLY capable teacher in the school.

"She just gives out the worksheets and tells us to do them. And we don't know how because she never explained them."

"Have you asked her to explain?"

"Yeah, but then she just gets all mad and yells at us. After the test, when everyone failed, then she gets up and explains the math. After we already failed."

Mrs. Parks's classroom routine was no secret, yet Lowrey would still listen. His ego, I think, needed constant approval in whatever form available. He cultivated the students' dependency, probably because he wanted them to need him as much as he needed them.

*He probably
wanted students
to need him
as much as he
needed them.*

One Friday, Daverrell Clifton, one of the "Lowrey Babies," had broken several of my class rules by leaving the room and letting a truant student into the building through a locked side door. After school, I tracked down Daverrell in Lowrey's room, doing his homework.

"Mr. Lowrey. Did Daverrell tell you what happened today in class?"

"No. What?"

As I related the story to Lowrey, he slowly sighed, closed his eyes, and nodded his head deliberately. To Daverrell, he said, "Have you gotten stupider since last year?"

"No."

"I think you have. Last year, when you were in my class, you never pulled any junk like that. Why is that?"

"I don't know."

"It's because you must have gotten stupider since last year. Why else would you behave in my class, last year, and this year you're screwing up in Mr. Rubinstein's class?"

Daverrell said nothing, yet the reason could be heard, echoing in his silence: Because Lowrey must be a better

teacher than Rubinstein. Because Daverrell could only
behave in a class led by Lowrey. Because Daverrell was lost
without Lowrey.

After watching Lowrey, I resolved to help students
claim the power, and accountability, for their education. I
began by refusing to listen to complaints about other teachers. I would cut them off by saying, "Don't tell me. I don't
want to know." This, however, didn't cure their disease. It
only suppressed a symptom. Besides, "Don't tell me" had a
"wink-wink" subtext that could be interpreted dangerously.
It was like saying, "I agree that your teacher stinks, but as a
colleague I shouldn't be having a discussion with you about
it."

*Students need
to claim the
power, and
accountability,
for their
education.*

I started trying to redirect the focus to the student and
what he or she could do to improve the situation.

"Have you been reading the textbook?" I would ask.

"He doesn't even assign any reading."

"He didn't tell you *not* to read the textbook, did he?"

"No."

"So, there you go. There is something that you can do.
Read the book. Just like you will in college. In college, the
professors present so much material in their lectures that
you have to go home and figure out most of it yourself.
Which is good, since when you learn it that way, you
remember it better."

When the second semester began, I had acquired two
classes of Algebra II and had lost my Algebra I classes. After
homeroom, Damon Robinson, one of my top Algebra I students, located me in my new room.

"They switched me out of your class."

"I know. I'm not teaching Algebra I this term."

"They gave me Mrs. Parks. I won't learn in that class."

"Yes you will. Just pay attention."

"But she doesn't explain. All she says is, 'Look up on the board. Do it like the sample problem.'"

"Do it like the sample problem? That's good advice. That's pretty much how you did it in my class."

"Yeah, but you explained."

"You weren't even listening most of the time."

"That's true. Because that stuff was so easy."

"What'd you get in here?"

"A 90."

"You won't have any trouble in there."

"But it's because you're a good teacher."

"It had nothing to do with me. You learned it by looking at the examples. So as long as you have a few sample problems, you'll be O.K."

"But if I need it, will you help me?"

"Yeah."

After that, Damon did stop by occasionally. And he came with many questions: Did I go to any clubs over the weekend? Did I get any phone numbers from the ladies? He was full of questions on many topics.

Except math.

*Redirect the
focus to what
the student can
do to improve
the situation.*

Answers
From
Real
Teachers

Classroom management is an individual and personal subject

Answers From Real Teachers

I have always liked it when books on challenging subjects
end with a section of answers to problems posed throughout
the book. For a subject as individual and personal as classroom management, however, there *are* no definitive answers.
Still, there are answers that have worked for different individuals.

For this last chapter, I asked an assortment of teachers I
respect to respond to two questions:

- *With regard to classroom management, what has worked for
  you?*
- *What advice would you give to other teachers?*

So I wouldn't bias their contributions, I didn't give most
of them an opportunity to read what I had written. Consequently, there are some interesting similarities in our opinions, as well as some contradictions.

The following teachers or former teachers gave their
advice:

- *Gambrill Hollister* is a fellow TFA alum of mine. Known
  for her kindness, intelligence, and organization, she
  proved that a petite and nice 22-year-old could handle
  even the toughest classes.

Answers

There ARE no definitive answers when it comes to classroom management.

- *Dave Berra* is his own worst discipline problem. A 24-year teaching veteran, he is known for his sharp wit and animated style. A mentor to many of the new teachers who start at his school, Berra has been able to keep his classes fresh by embracing change.

- *Lauralyn Lonquist* and *Celeste Hill* are a duo from a middle school where I taught. Whenever I sat in the lounge complaining about how I couldn't get five consecutive minutes of silence, one of them was sure to frustrate me by saying, "Ewwww. I hate it when they're quiet." In a school of nearly 3000 adolescents, they were known for making class fun while still maintaining control — quite an accomplishment.

- *Cheri Thurston* is my brilliant editor. Though I have never had the privilege of seeing her teach, I know that if she taught as well as she plays the accordion and writes books, plays, poetry and musicals, then her classes were a real treat.

- *Scott Murphy* knows the rules of management so well that he also knows when those rules can be broken. This guitar-playing, folk-singing, shorts-wearing favorite has mastered the balance between being yourself and being in control.

  Read on to see what these individuals have to say about classroom management.

Advice from real teachers

Like your students. I think the most important thing for any new teacher to remember is to like your students, genuinely. Enjoy them. Laugh with them. Appreciate them.

Most students are easy to love. A few aren't, especially if they are giving you problems in class. If you find yourself starting to dislike a student, stop, before the feeling takes hold. If you allow the dislike to develop, the student will always know. You can't convincingly pretend to like a student you don't like.

Find any excuse to talk to the student about something — anything — other than school. I would sometimes ask a student about his T-shirt (What kind of music does that group play?) or ask her opinion about something (So tell me: Are you a cat person or a dog person?) or ask for information ("What's for lunch today? Was it any good, or should I go ahead and eat the peanut butter sandwich I brought?) It doesn't matter much what you find to talk about, as long as it will help you see the student as a real person.

Of course, it helps if you are able to work in the conversation casually, perhaps during group work, or even if a student is in your room for detention. It is not terribly effective to approach the child as if you are saying, "All right. I'm here to bond with you. Let's chat. Tell me your innermost feelings."

This method has almost always worked for me. Once I can see a student as someone's little boy or girl, instead of "that kid in the back of the room with the smart mouth," I almost always manage to see the student differently — and to

If you find yourself starting to dislike a student, stop.

begin to genuinely like the person I see. It makes all the difference in the world.

Be prepared. From the very first day of school on, I always shut the door as the bell is ringing and immediately begin class, working every single minute of class until the dismissal bell. I want my students to feel as I feel — that the material to be covered is important and we don't have time to mess around. I know the goals I want to accomplish in that period, and I make sure that I have all of my supplies and information in order to accomplish those goals.

Students know when their teacher is not organized and prepared, and they do not appreciate the lack of effort. Part of the preparation is helping students understand the relevance of the work they are asked to do in class, to understand that even though they may have little interest in the subject, they are learning something that matters. If they don't believe it is important, then the class is a waste of their time. They have a perfect opportunity to relieve some stress and boredom by acting inappropriately.

Attach yourself to a master teacher. Find someone who is an excellent teacher and who is willing to share ideas with you. Don't be ashamed to say, "I don't know how to do this. Help me." Most truly successful teachers are just that — teachers. They love to teach anyone, even another teacher. Find another teacher to bounce ideas off of, to unburden yourself on, to emulate in areas where you have trouble.

Reward positive behavior. Positive reinforcement does work. My favorite way to reward positive behavior is with a lottery.

Don't be ashamed to say, "I don't know how to do this. Help me."

For any uncalled-for good deed a student performs (such as helping another student with an assignment or staying to help me clean up after a lab), or for any grade higher than 90, I pass out a preprinted lottery card. The student writes his or her name on the card, and the card goes into a shoe box for the whole semester.

Each Friday, right before the final bell, I draw three to five cards, and the lucky winners draw from a box for a prize of extra credit, a tardy pass, candy or (the favorite) a batch of chocolate chip cookies. Not only does this encourage Friday attendance, but it means all students have to be in their seats and quiet at the end of class on Friday.

Despite the fact that my students are "too cool" high schoolers, they love this. I use the tickets to reward students who don't do so well academically but who, once in a while, do a good deed. After they figure it out, more and more students try to show me how good they can be and, at least in some classes, some of the social norms change a little.

Okay, so it is blatant bribery, but it works! The student who wins the cookies each week sometimes asks me to keep them until the end of the day so he or she won't have to share them with everyone else in the hall who sees the tell-tale brown paper bag. Others use the cookies as a way to reward people who are nice to them.

In three years, I have baked more than 7,000 chocolate chip cookies. It has been well worth the effort.

For good deeds and good grades, enter students' names into a lottery.

Develop lessons that allow kids to be themselves.
Students love to argue, to have some of their own opinions validated, to move around, to be outrageous, to touch things. I once saw a PBS show about training killer whales. The narrator said that training the animals merely requires

getting them to do what they naturally do, but on cue. I try to do the same thing in the classroom.

Be creative. Not every teacher can think of creative ways to present a subject. That is no excuse for having a dull class. One hour can seem an eternity to the poor students trapped with the boring teacher who does the exact same thing everyday.

   I am very organized, but I had to learn to be creative. I learned from other teachers. I would tell them what the topic was, and they would offer wonderful ideas on how to present it. It often takes a lot of time to plan a class with interesting manipulatives and different teaching techniques, but students appreciate the effort and repay their teacher by staying on task and behaving appropriately.

Show respect. When teachers sit at their desks grading papers when they should be working with students, the students feel ignored and unimportant. (These teachers are often the ones who have the most discipline problems.) Students deserve to be recognized, and they deserve to be treated with respect.

   I use a wall of my classroom for a bulletin board that reads, "You may not be great in English class, BUT YOU ARE GREAT AT SOMETHING." It lists all kinds of activities and subjects, such as running, computers, sewing, diving, mathematics, singing, swimming, painting, repairing cars, typing, etc. It is a reminder to the kids and myself that people have different talents. It is a reminder that everyone deserves respect.

When teachers sit at their desks grading papers, students feel ignored and unimportant.

Remember what it felt like to be a kid. Try to remember your own days in school. What frustrated you? What pleased you? If you can remember those feelings, you can understand and connect with your students so much better.

Don't forget to smile. I was so nervous my first semester of teaching that, almost without thinking, I failed to smile. In fact, when I allowed my class to have a Halloween party I remember one of the students actually saying to her friend, "Wow! She's smiling! She laughed at that joke!"

That made me stop and think. I have always been known as someone with a low amusement threshold (I laugh at anything), and even at the young age of 21, I already had smile wrinkles. But I was so focused on keeping my kids in line that I had a hard time also being nice to them and enjoying teaching. After the Halloween comment, I realized what a hardnose I had been. I spent the rest of the year trying to be nicer and figuring out how to do that without losing control — not an easy task.

Find your own style. For every teacher whose "way" is held up as a model, there is an equally effective instructor who gets the same results with a totally different style and manner of teaching. It is important for teachers to understand that there is no perfect way to handle a class.

One year I taught in a classroom that was separated from the next room by double French doors. The teacher in the other room was a good friend, and we could pass freely into each other's room – and so could sound. After a particularly noisy class period, I complained to him that I seemed to have no classroom discipline. He looked at me, puzzled, and replied. "You know, your class was perfectly quiet. You

There is no perfect way to handle a class.

127

broke the silence by bugging students with inane questions about their families, their extracurricular activities and last night's TV."

It was then that I realized I was my own worst enemy. I had read about quiet classes; I have even seen some — kids in neat rows silently answering end-of-chapter questions. I remember thinking, "How boring!" I have since come to accept that the quiet class can work for some teachers, but not me.

A teacher friend describes my class as "organized chaos." I like that! Quietude deafens me. My classroom reflects me and my large Italian family upbringing — lots of smiling, arguing, arm waving, kidding, activity. I have found my own style, my own voice. It works for me.

The finest teachers are consistent. They are consistently unpredictable.

Be consistent. The finest teachers are consistent. They may be harsh, comical, stern or methodical. They may even be unpredictable, but they are consistently unpredictable. A good teacher does not sway from rules or ideals and is unwavering in his approach. The students are not forced to guess who the teacher is. They know. When they have that person again their senior year, they know. When their brother or sister gets that teacher, they know, too.

Be in charge. Understand that kids want you to be in charge. When I first started teaching, I worried that students would hate me after I "yelled" at them about something. (I'm not a yeller. By "yell" I really mean giving them a no nonsense "talking to.") In fact, the first time I really came down hard on a student, I dreaded seeing him the next day. I was afraid he would be so angry he would try harder to make my life miserable.

To my surprise, he bounced into class the next day with a chirpy, "Hi," and that was that.

I soon discovered that kids expect to be yelled at now and then. In fact, I often got the feeling that — if too much time had passed since I had given a class a "talking to" — they would do something to precipitate one. It seemed as though it made them feel safe, as if they had to check and verify that, "Yep. She's still the one in charge."

I observed this phenomenon with every class of young people I ever taught. Every now and then — not often — I would have to become stern and give them a lecture about something or other, just because they seemed to need it and expect it in order to calm themselves down. It is as though they wanted to shape up but just needed a little help.

It is important not to think of yourself as a failure if you have to get "on" the kids now and then. It may, in fact, be a sign that you are succeeding.

Kids WANT the teacher to be in charge.

Don't teach just to pay the bills. Have fun with teaching. Enjoy it. If you don't, move on to something you do enjoy.

I love going to school and teaching kids. I like to be in charge of people, directing, teaching, demonstrating. I like to see people progress in their skills. That gives me satisfaction. Seriously, some days I don't even know it is payday. My check will sit in my box until the following Monday because I sometimes forget that what I am doing is a job.

Keep learning. Always remember to keep on learning new things yourself. That way you don't stagnate. You have fresh excitement for your topics, and you can communicate that excitement to your students.

*Students love
the drama of an
argument.*

Don't argue. It is a big mistake to be sucked into an argument with a student in front of the class. You will lose, even if you technically win the argument.

The same instinct that causes kids to rush down the halls toward the scene of a fight (often to egg on the participants) also makes them love the drama of an argument between a student and a teacher. The student you are arguing with will "perform" for his audience, i.e., the class members, who will almost always root for one of their own. The longer they keep the argument going, the longer they avoid getting back to work. It's almost as though, in an argument with a student, the teacher is the puppet, and the kids are pulling the strings. Class time is wasted, and nothing is gained.

Refuse to argue about rules or the merit of something you are doing or the "fairness" of what you have done. Refusing to argue does not mean that you are unreasonable or tyrannical or won't listen to kids. In fact, I always explain that I will listen carefully to a student's case — if she talks to me calmly after class or makes her points in a letter. I also point out that I have changed my mind many times when students present a good case.

The result? Very few students really stay to discuss a matter when they don't have an audience to back them up. Those who do stay usually do have a good point, and I generally act on their suggestions.

Recognize what you get out of teaching. Why do I teach? Quite simply, I do it for me. Teaching fills needs in me: the need to interact with people, to show off my intelligence, to be held in high regard, to entertain, to affect change. Granted, this doesn't sound very altruistic, but I'm not at cross-purposes with my students' needs. My students and I enjoy a symbiotic relationship. I like to entertain; they like to be entertained. I like to interact with people; they like to interact with me. I like to cause change; they hate the status quo. Finally, I like to share information; they like receiving information. In the end, we both benefit, and school remains exciting.

A failed lesson here and there does no harm to students.

See students as individuals. I once read an article that said a good teacher must understand his students' culture —African-American, Hispanic, Vietnamese, etc. Although helpful, this understanding is not an end in itself. Rather, it provides a backdrop to real cultural understanding – the culture of the individual.

I teach kids, each one as distinct as a fingerprint. It is important and necessary for teaching, and for classroom management, to know as much as possible about each individual student. That's why I talk to students every day before, during and after class. When students are doing some sponge activities at the beginning of class, I check roll by calling each student's name and saying something to each one ("How's your brother?" or "Nice game yesterday.") The more I learn about a student, the better teacher I become.

Take chances. If a teacher shuts his door and does a good job, he will be left alone. I like to experiment, and I know a couple of failed lessons a year does no harm to students. Also, I don't ask administrators if my lessons are acceptable beforehand. My motto is "Do it until you're told to stop."

Answers

Teachers who add "Okay?" to every request sound wimpy.

Work on your "delivery." All teachers should tape record (or videotape) themselves teaching now and then. How they speak to a group really does make a difference.

For example, many teachers add the tag question "Okay?" after everything they tell kids to do, as if they are afraid of making a demand or request and want to soften it, or they don't want to sound too bossy. The result is that (a) they sound wimpy and (b) they invite a response from the child, like "No." It is important for teachers to state firmly what they want the student to do, as if there is no question that, of course, the child will do what is requested.

Another thing that can make a teacher sound wimpy is the now trendy "talking in questions" voice inflection. It has become so pervasive that many teachers don't even know they have it. It sounds something like this:

The worksheet I passed out yesterday on verbs? You need to turn it in by the end of the period today? And be sure your name is in the upper right-hand corner? And be sure you wrote in complete sentences and in ink?

People in positions of authority sound weak and tentative when they adopt this habit. Try imagining a leader like a company president or a general using the "question" style of speech:

I've been looking over our budget? We need to cut costs? So I'm going to have to lay some people off? So you need to prepare yourselves for some bad news?

Or

We're going to, like, invade South Lumbago? So I need you to prepare yourself for battle? Okay?

By listening to themselves on tape, new teachers can see if they have unconsciously adopted this increasingly popular style of speech — or other bad speech habits that may be undermining their effectiveness.

Be honest with students. I am painfully honest with my students about everything, including myself. As adults, we recognize patronizing or pretentious people. So do students. They know "phony," and they hate it.

Being honest doesn't have to mean you share everything. Being honest can include saying, "That's not a question I want to answer," or "That's personal."

Take advantage of the teachable moment.
Although lesson plan forms were developed by administrators for administrators, planning is essential for classroom survival. You have to know where you have been and where you are going. However, lesson plans are not written in indelible ink; they can be changed in an instant to allow for the greatest of all teaching experiences: the teachable moment. A teachable moment is a spontaneous lesson usually generated by something a student says, something that is often only peripherally related to the planned lesson.

Let me give one example. I was introducing the Greek tragedy Medea with some background information. Suddenly a student remarked that the story about Jason and his uncle was just like *The Lion King*. Before long, other students were pointing out similarities between the two stories. A teachable moment! The lesson changed from introducing Medea to making connections between literary classics and modern cartoons. Unplanned moments make learning relevant and

The greatest of all teaching experiences is the "teachable moment."

fun. A good teacher needs only be open-minded enough —
and flexible enough — to recognize them when they occur.

Don't teach summer school. Do not, I repeat, do not
teach summer school. Any teacher needs a break, a chance
to recharge, to unwind. Summer vacation is the only real
perk of teaching. Don't give it away easily. Spend your summers traveling, working odd jobs, sunbathing or even watching grass grow — anything except teaching. Trust me; without a break, you will burn out.

You can only give so much.

*Every teacher
needs a chance
to recharge and
unwind.*

Ten Years Later

Things are not always as simple as they seem

Looking back...

It's been ten years since the publication of this book and nearly twenty since my harrowing first year of teaching. For this new edition, I've had the opportunity to reflect again on my experiences as a developing teacher.

Today, I have a different perspective on what happened during those first two years. When I wrote originally, I was still relatively close in time to those first few years and my interpretation was somewhat skewed by what I *wanted* those years to be like. The way I wrote it, I was too nice my first year, too mean the second year, and then, apparently, "just right" afterwards. Now I have a more realistic view of what it was really like (kind of like looking down from a hot-air balloon; the further away you get, the more you can see.)

Things were a lot more complicated than the picture I painted. My first year was so distressing that, looking back, I'm convinced I suffered from a type of post-traumatic stress disorder. Although I know the experiences aren't comparable at all, I've read memoirs by Vietnam War veterans and found myself thinking, "Been there." My twenty-year obsession with reliving and trying to undo my first year failure demonstrates that I still haven't completely gotten over it.

It would take a lot of time and a lot of distance for me to truly escape what I lived through. That's why, after my fifth year of teaching, I quit.

A new career

Programming was the opposite of teaching. I liked the fact that the computers, though often disobedient, never talked back.

In 1996, I left teaching and pursued a degree in computer science. I spent the next five years sitting at a desk talking only to a computer in a language called "C++."

Programming was the opposite of teaching. I liked the fact that the computers, though often disobedient, never talked back. If a computer became impossible to work with, I wouldn't think twice about doing the equivalent of a *One Flew Over The Cuckoo's Nest* frontal lobotomy by wiping clean the contents of the hard drive. The best part about being a computer programmer was that, unlike being a teacher, I didn't have to take anything home with me—not papers, not emotions.

As a beginning computer programmer, I started with one of the most tedious and uncreative assignments. I was a level one debugger for a desktop publishing program. Commercial software, I learned, is generally released with thousands of errors or "bugs." Though a team of testers tries to find them before the software is shipped, many bugs still slip by. Home users, who pay $500 for the privilege of using the crash-prone programs, locate the remaining bugs and call the company to complain.

When enough calls are logged about the same problem, a debugger is notified. Back then, I'd read the heading of the "bug report"—something like, "Program crashes when you push enter, backspace, and shift at the same time while saving a file." It was not my place to ask why anyone would ever find themselves doing that, let alone take time to report the bug, but dozens did. The first step in fixing a bug was to make sure it wasn't a false alarm. I'd push this ridiculous combination of keys in an attempt to crash the program. I always feared that one day I'd see a bug report reading, "Program abruptly closes when user sticks the mouse up his nose."

If I could successfully crash the program by following the steps, I'd have to comb through a million lines of computer code to fix it. Otherwise, I'd close out the bug with the three-word explanation, "Unable to reproduce." Ironically, this was also an accurate description of my social life at the time.

Not like teaching at all. When I was a teacher, I was always looking at my watch and thinking, "How did this period go by so quickly?" As a programmer, I would do the opposite. Ten times a day, I'd estimate the time and then compare it to the actual time. If the real time was significantly later than the time I thought it was, I'd get a little thrill.

Another way I'd make the time go by more quickly was with something I could never do as a teacher—use the bathroom. At the slightest hint of discomfort, I'd be off to the bathroom for a ten-minute break. On the way back, I'd stop by the cooler and refill my water bottle, in anticipation of my next bathroom break.

Still, I never completely separated myself from teaching. At night, I taught computer programming at a college. Over the summers, I continued volunteering at teacher training programs, presenting the ideas from this book. I was a teacher in a computer programmer's unstylish clothing.

The main result of my five agonizing years as a debugger was that I became much more marketable. Even though I hated being a computer programmer, I thought that if I could land a job in the financial district of Manhattan, I could at least make a lot of money while hating it.

When I was a teacher, I was always looking at my watch and thinking, "How did this period go by so quickly?" As a programmer, I would do the opposite.

Moving to Manhattan

Teacher 1991-1996

*For five years,
I had embraced
the Teach For
America motto,
"All children
can learn."*

The words above look more like something carved on a tombstone than a line from a resume. At first, the details of my accomplishments during my five years of teaching dominated my resume. My employment recruiter kept shortening the description of my teaching experience, arguing that it would only hurt my chance of getting an offer to program computers for a Fortune 500 investment firm.

I refused his request that I cut my teaching experience out of the resume altogether, but I compromised by allowing it to become one line. For five years, I had embraced the Teach For America motto, "All children can learn." I had worked hard to show that, with high expectations, all children not only can but will learn. Just as I would never cut those experiences from my memory, I couldn't disrespect them by cutting them completely out of my resume.

When I moved to New York in August of 2001, my recruiter, Mark, set up a series of job interviews for me. My last interview took place on the 38th floor of the North Tower of the World Trade Center. The date was September 10, 2001. Had they offered me the job and asked how soon I could start, I surely would have said "tomorrow."

On September 13, two days after the tragic events at the World Trade Center, my headhunter called me. Casually, he asked, "Did you get a chance to write a thank you letter to the people at Lehman Brothers?"

I was incredulous. "Do you really think I should, under the circumstances?" I asked.

"Oh, definitely. Nobody died from that floor. They've even set up new headquarters in the Marriott hotel in midtown."

My pass for an interview at the World Trade Center

My last interview took place on the 38th floor of the North Tower of the World Trade Center. The date was September 10, 2001.

Not knowing what could possibly be appropriate, I wrote an e-mail to the man who had interviewed me: "I was relieved to learn that everyone on the 38th floor evacuated the building safely. I'm not sure if the attacks have changed your need for computer consultants, but I'd like you to know that I really enjoyed our interview and am still eager to work for you."

He never got back to me.

Teaching of a different kind

*I enjoyed
training new
teachers and
knowing
that I was,
once again,
making a
difference,
though
indirectly.*

September 11 definitely took the momentum out of my new life plan to be a wealthy computer programmer in Manhattan. Just as ten years earlier I hadn't been able to muster up the energy to complete my law school applications, now I wasn't actively pursuing computer jobs.

In early 2002, I learned of a job opening with the New York City Teaching Fellows (NYCTF). NYCTF is a spin-off of the Teach For America program that trained me. While the Teach For America program recruits recent college graduates who want to teach for a few years before pursing other higher-paying careers, NYCTF does the opposite. It recruits people who have already had lucrative jobs and are now ready to become teachers.

I took the teacher training position, and my passion for teaching was instantly renewed. I enjoyed training new teachers and knowing that I was, once again, making a difference, though indirectly. Those twenty teachers would be teaching a total of three thousand kids. By helping them become better teachers, I would help those three thousand kids learn more, without ever meeting them.

One of the connections I made during this time gave my name to Danny Jaye, the math department chair at Stuyvesant High School in Manhattan. Stuyvesant had recently been featured on the front page of *Newsweek* as "The High School At Ground Zero," since it was located only three blocks from the infamous disaster. A teacher who was concerned about the air quality in the school had requested a transfer, Jaye explained. A man who likes to get right to the

point, he asked, "How would you like to teach in the best
high school in the city?"

For many teachers, this would be a dream come true.
For me, it was a serious dilemma. In my Teach For America
years, the low teacher pay was balanced by the knowledge
that I was making a difference for some very needy kids.
Though some Stuyvesant students were definitely trauma-
tized by their sudden evacuation on September 11, they
were not academically needy. I had a once-in-a-lifetime
opportunity to teach at Stuyvesant, the most competitive
math and science school in New York City, but deep down
I knew I belonged in the low-performing schools in nearby
Bedford-Stuyvesant, the area featured in Spike Lee's *Do The
Right Thing.*

Despite my concerns, I agreed. If nothing else, I figured
that the job would be easy. *Why* I thought that is a mystery.

When I taught before, I had been so obsessed with my
work that teaching seemed almost like a drug. I'm sure that
when I told my family about my decision, they whispered
behind my back, "Oh, God, he's teaching again." If you've
ever been a teacher, you're always a teacher. It's like being
an alcoholic. Even when you're not teaching, you're still a
teacher. You're just a teacher in recovery.

But what concerned me most wasn't the daunting task
of planning lessons, making tests, and grading homework. It
was something more practical: Did I still have the ability to
"hold it in?" My time-wasting habit of using the bathroom
anytime I was bored had completely ruined my former bathroom stamina.

Teaching the "bad kids." Stuyvesant High School occu-
pied a ten-floor building in downtown Manhattan and was

*Even when
you're not
teaching,
you're still
a teacher.
You're just
a teacher
in recovery.*

at that time the most expensive school ever built, at about one hundred and fifty million dollars. With marble floors and an Olympic-sized pool, this building had the best of everything. Twenty thousand of the top eighth graders in the five boroughs of Manhattan take the placement exam every November to see which eight hundred will be admitted to this school.

Of my five scheduled classes, three were trigonometry classes and two were something called "advanced algebra." Though the "advanced" in the title makes it sound like an accelerated class, I soon learned that this course is reserved for the lowest performing eleventh graders at Stuyvesant, students who were deemed not ready for precalculus.

I wasn't intimidated. The worst kids at the most competitive school in the state, I figured, are still better than the best kids anywhere else. What were the "bad kids" at this prestigious school going to do that was so bad? Carve math equations into their desks with the point of their compasses?

Yet, when I met the students, they lived up to their reputation. "We're the stupid class," Dorian announced to me on my first day. Half the class strolled in late and five were absent. Most of the students didn't have notebooks or textbooks. Some were sleeping. Though they were not stupid, they were unmotivated. I realized that in any group of students, some have to be the weakest. With group dynamics, those are the kids who will act out. The low expectations that these student experienced in advanced algebra had become a self-fulfilling prophecy.

There was no way I was going to allow a group of Stuyvesant students to walk all over me, even if they were deemed incorrigible. I quickly assessed the situation and

What were the "bad kids" at this prestigious school going to do that was so bad? Carve math equations into their desks with the point of their compasses?

called upon the skills I had written about in this book: Never make threats. Keep your cool. Keep them busy with work. Call parents without warning.

Within a week, I had the class behaving. Next I had to get them learning.

I decided to do something a little bit creative. We were studying graphs, so I told them that I had gone to a party over the weekend and spent the entire time making a graph of the number of people who were at the party at each successive minute. I then passed out a copy of the graph and had students write a story about what might have happened at the party.

One student wrote a story that had everyone creeped out by the dork in the corner (me) counting during the party. In the story, the police eventually come and take him away for trespassing, forcing him to endure a cavity search. Because the details of his story coincided exactly with the ups and downs of the graph, I gave the student a score of 100 on the assignment.

A fun lesson like that entitles a teacher to two weeks of being boring, which I took advantage of as I taught them how to form intricate curves from complicated equations. I was on my way to taming the dreaded advanced algebra students.

At the end of the year I passed out a questionnaire for students to give me feedback about the course. One student wrote, "I used to feel dumb in math, and now I think I'm smart again. Thanks."

It turns out that all children can learn—even the "bad" kids at Stuyvesant.

One student wrote, "I used to feel dumb in math, and now I think I'm smart again. Thanks."

Ten Years Later

Discipline is only in the background of my mind now, and I can focus on other issues that make teaching rewarding.

Eight years later. Eight years later, I'm still teaching at Stuyvesant. Now a veteran member of the staff, I've gotten to experience many things I missed out on in my short stints at other schools. I've gotten to participate in creating new courses and revising curricula. I've gotten to take a homeroom of freshmen from their first day as timid ninth graders all the way through to reading their names at their graduation.

Discipline is only in the background of my mind now, and I can focus on other issues that make teaching rewarding.

Even though I got into teaching by accident, I now think my decision to pursue teaching was more than just a whim. I think it is what I was meant to do.

Reassessing the past

When I wrote *Reluctant Disciplinarian* in 1999, I was concerned that five years of teaching might not qualify me as an expert. Looking back ten years later, I'm now glad I wrote the book when I did. Had I waited until I was a seasoned veteran (i.e. "old"), I might have been too far removed from the memories of my first year. The hard edges of the stories might have become softened by time.

I was able to easily outline my advice because back then, I was still in the process of fighting my instincts in the classroom. I was keenly aware of my moment to moment management decisions. By now, I've internalized most of my own advice. Most of my management decisions now occur automatically, in my subconscious. This has made me better at teaching math, but worse at teaching teachers.

Although this book is often described as a humorous memoir, it's important to remember that my first year was *not* funny when it was happening. I did my best to pick the parts that could be described in a funny way and to write about those. By the time I told about some of the disturbing incidents, such as picking up a desk with a student in it or screaming into a kid's ear until I collapsed, I hoped that readers were in a laughing mood. I hoped they were willing to overlook the fact that I was doing things that should have gotten me fired.

Possible misinterpretations. Over the years, I have sometimes worried that in trying to keep *Reluctant Disciplinarian* pithy, I may have failed to thoroughly explain some of

Most of my management decisions now occur automatically, in my subconscious. This has made me better at teaching math, but worse at teaching teachers.

the more vital points, which could be open to misinterpretation.

For example, one of my most important pieces of advice is, "Start with traditional methods." Traditional methods generally include worksheets and answering questions at the end of a chapter. Students expect such things and thus are reassured that a new teacher is a "real" teacher when he or she gives such assignments.

However, I've come to understand that one of the reasons such methods work in the beginning is that it is very clear to students what they are supposed to do. A clear lesson is less frustrating for students, producing fewer discipline issues. And when students are doing something clear, they are more likely to learn. That gives them confidence in the teacher and in themselves.

*But using
"traditional
methods" does
not mean that
you stand
in front
of a lectern
reading from
your notes
while students
copy furiously.*

But using "traditional methods" does not mean that you stand in front of a lectern reading from your notes while students copy furiously. Traditional methods can still include interaction with students, questioning, discussion, and guided and independent work.

In other words, I'm not saying that a new teacher should be completely boring, just partially boring.

When can you be "fun"? Safe lessons help you maintain both student confidence and student order. But if you play it too safe, you risk losing the most important part of teaching—a deep learning experience.

The goal of teaching is to get students to think. Because of my inability during my first year to manage my students, the only critical thinking that ever happened was when a kid screamed, "This class sucks."

But how long, exactly, should you wait to try something more involved, and how creative should you allow yourself to be? Unfortunately, there is no formula.

Even in my second year of teaching, when I tried to take as few risks as possible, I did create some less traditional lessons. After my first month, the students trusted me and were willing to give more creative activities a chance. They also appreciated, I think, that I was willing to take the time to try to make math a little more interesting for them. Every few weeks I would do something "fun." These activities required a lot of planning since I wanted the students to feel that they learned from them.

One project I developed was a week-long unit about how to balance checkbooks, using positive and negative numbers. I went to the bank and got blank checkbooks for each student and created a society where students owned businesses and other students would write them checks, and they all had to balance their checkbooks with positive and negative numbers.

Three days into the project, I had to abandon it. It was a disaster. There were hundreds of checks passed around and I, as the banker, had not created a good system for keeping track of them. Still, the students did not hold this against me. I went back to my more traditional approach for another two weeks before again trying to do something a little different.

Playing it safe does serve a purpose, but you don't want to stunt your professional growth by playing it too safe. It's true that every time you plan something a little out there, you are taking a risk. But after a few weeks of successful management, don't let fear prevent you from becoming the most effective teacher you can be. If you've done your job in establishing that you are a real teacher, you can overcome the occasional lesson dud.

If you've done your job in establishing that you are a real teacher, you can overcome the occasional lesson dud.

Teachers in the movies

It's unlikely that a movie based on *Reluctant Disciplinarian* will ever be made. The story arc is all wrong. Here's what it should be to fit the pattern most teacher movies follow:

The problem is that unrealistic portrayals of what it takes to be a great teacher make great real-life teachers look bad.

- First year teacher is almost run out of the building on the first day.
- First year teacher wins over the class with a creative lesson.
- First year teacher wins over the bad kid with unconditional love.
- First year teacher leads class to amazing academic progress.

Stories like this are dramatically more satisfying than mine. In my story, the teacher doesn't win over his first year students at all, though he learns enough to succeed with a different group of students his second year. This doesn't fit the teacher movie pattern at all.

The problem is that unrealistic portrayals of what it takes to be a great teacher make great real-life teachers look bad. The public sees teacher movies and believes them.

New teachers have also seen these movies and can be influenced, perhaps subconsciously, by the lessons of these films. To see what new teachers might learn from teacher movies, I recently re-watched four of the most famous teacher movies: *Blackboard Jungle*, *Dangerous Minds*, *Freedom Writers*, and *Stand and Deliver*.

Let me first review the basic story lines in these movies.

Blackboard Jungle. In *Blackboard Jungle* (1955), new teacher Richard Dadier takes on a group of tough boys (including Sidney Poitier, later to become Mr. Thackeray in *To Sir, with Love*) at a vocational school. He stays committed in spite of getting beaten up by his students in a dark alley. Students eventually send a series of notes to his wife claiming Dadier is having an affair with another teacher. The stress induced by these notes causes his wife to go into premature labor, and she nearly loses the baby. Although he wins over the leader of the class, Dadier doesn't have as much success with another student, who threatens him with a switchblade. He's saved by yet another student, who jabs the knife-wielding kid with an American flag.

She toughens up and inspires them with candy bars and lessons about drug-themed Bob Dylan songs.

Dangerous Minds. In *Dangerous Minds* (1995), Michelle Pfeiffer plays Louanne Johnson, a former marine who becomes a teacher in Los Angeles. On her first day, the kids call her "white bread" and throw papers at her. She toughens up and inspires them with candy bars and lessons about drug-themed Bob Dylan songs. Though she is successful, the emotional burden of being a teacher is too much for her, especially after one of her students is killed. She resigns, but her students convince her to stay.

Freedom Writers. In *Freedom Writers* (2007), Hilary Swank portrays the real Erin Gruwell, who rescues a class filled with angry ninth grade gang members, played by 25-year-old actors. After failing to win them over with rap music, she gets their attention by teaching them about the Holocaust. Their journals, written in those black marble composition notebooks, are eventually published as *The Freedom Writers Diary*.

The harmony she fosters in her class inspires a girl to testify against her own boyfriend for shooting the boyfriend of another girl in the class. Gruwell petitions the school board to permit her to continue teaching her students for all four years of high school and then, according to the postscript at the end of the movie, she leaves the high school to teach in the college that some of her students attend.

Though humor is a tool that effective teachers do use, they know when it is inappropriate.

Stand and Deliver. *Stand and Deliver* (1988) is based on the true story of math teacher Jaime Escalante. In two years he guides a group of eighteen students who hardly know fractions to pass the advanced placement calculus test. Later the Educational Testing Service calls into question their scores. Outraged, the students agree to retake the test at the end of the summer, to prove themselves. They all pass.

Here are some misguided lessons I've learned from these movies about teachers:

Myth # 1: You should be funny. On Escalante's first day of teaching, a girl asks "Can we talk about sex?" He responds with, "If we talk about sex, I have to assign sex for homework." In *Blackboard Jungle*, Mr. Dadier reacts to a baseball that barely misses his head when his back is turned, "Whoever threw that ball, you'll never pitch for the Yankees."

Though humor is a tool that effective teachers do use, they know when it is inappropriate. Teachers make up funny examples to illustrate their points and make them more memorable, but they don't joke after a student has made a very inappropriate comment or when they have been assaulted.

Myth #2: You should be physically tough. In *Dangerous Minds*, Louanne Johnson takes control of her class on the second day by donning a leather jacket and writing on the board "I am a U.S. Marine." She then teaches the students some karate moves, and when the kids are trying them out says, "You don't know shit." In *Stand and Deliver*, Jaime Escalante asks the tough kid the question, "What is negative two plus two?" When the kid refuses to answer, Escalante whispers, "I'll snap your neck like a toothpick."

Real teachers are tough, in a way, but the toughness is more mental than physical. Making physical threats to a student will likely get you fired, and even if it doesn't, it will not scare your students into cooperation.

Real teachers are tough, in a way, but the toughness is more mental than physical.

Myth #3: A creative lesson can win over your class. Richard Dadier shows his class a cartoon, which students then discuss on a high level. Louanne Johnson creates a contest that has students compare the poetry of Dylan Thomas with that of Bob Dylan. Erin Gruwell brings her students on a class trip to the Holocaust Museum. Jaime Escalante chops apples with a cleaver to illustrate fractions. These moments serve as turning points for each of the teachers.

I do like creative lessons, but they are not usually what really wins over a class. Creative lessons are often unstructured and confusing. After the students are finished with them, they are sometimes not really clear about what they learned. What wins over a class is a clear activity that has them practice a newly learned skill and then demonstrate to the teacher and themselves that they have mastered that skill.

*There are some
miserable
teachers out
there, but most
of them are
caring and
bright.*

Still, students do appreciate a well-planned creative lesson, and such a lesson serves another important purpose. It shows students that their teacher cares enough to try something a little different. In my classes, I do something fairly creative once a week, and once a month I try to do something completely crazy. At the end of the year when I survey the students about what they remember about the class, it's always those few wacky lessons. Twenty years from now, they'll probably "misremember" that I did lessons like that every day. But it will be the daily, ordinary lessons, I believe, that will have taught them the skills they most needed.

Myth #4: Many teachers and all administrators are evil. In *Dangerous Minds*, a student is murdered after he is sent away from the office for not knocking on the door. In *Freedom Writers*, the school's textbook storage area is off limits to Erin Gruwell, who is forced to take a second and third job in order to buy books for her class herself. She is also yelled at by another teacher who tells her, "You don't know the first thing about these kids. And you're not qualified to make judgments about the teachers who have to survive this place."

There are some miserable teachers out there, but most of them are caring and bright. Sometimes the complainers are the most dominant people in the lounge, so it feels like there are more of them. But teaching is hard, and people who are ignorant and miserable can generally find an easier way to make the same money. Many of them leave teaching to do something else.

I've taken a couple of jabs at administrators in this book. An unsupportive administrator can really make things difficult for a teacher. Some administrators are former bad teachers who got sick of the classroom. Some are former good teachers who, after spending too much time out of the classroom, have lost touch with reality. But many of the administrators I've known were good teachers and are also good administrators. Without the guidance of one of my administrators, Armando Alaniz, I surely would have quit during my first year.

Myth #5: To be a successful teacher you have to be a superhero. To give everything possible to her students, Erin Gruwell works three jobs and destroys her marriage. Jaime Escalante neglects his family by teaching sixty hours a week and also volunteers to teach night school to adults learning English. Louanne Johnson visits the homes of all her students.

These movies imply that to become an outstanding teacher, you have to give up the rest of your life. The fact is that almost anyone would burn out after one year if they really did all that the movie teachers do.

Dangerous Minds, Freedom Writers, and *Stand and Deliver* are all "based on" truth. In reality, there is usually a lot more to the truth than what we see in the movie. For example, Escalante's first calculus class consisted of five students who had been through a structured feeder pattern taught by Escalante and another teacher for four years. Hardly a new teacher, Escalante was in his eighth year, having taught groups of increasing size for three years before teaching the group of eighteen that was portrayed in the movie. The true story would make a dull movie. Every teaching movie based on truth has similar flaws.

These movies imply that to become an outstanding teacher, you have to give up the rest of your life.

*When teachers
watch movies
about teaching,
they have a
completely
different
experience
than someone
who has never
taught.*

The appeal of teacher movies. With all my experience
as a teacher, then, you might be surprised to learn that I
enjoy watching these flawed movies. The more I've thought
about it, the more I understand why.

I once saw the movie *The Count of Monte Cristo* with a
friend of mine who was in the process of writing her doc-
toral thesis on French novels of the nineteenth century. I
thought the movie was pretty good, but she didn't like it
since she had already read the twelve-hundred page book
numerous times—in its native French. Her main complaints
were that they changed the ending and that they left out
some of the best parts. For teachers, watching a movie about
teaching is like watching a movie where you have already
read the book in its native language.

When teachers watch movies about teaching, they have
a completely different experience than someone who has
never taught. They will laugh at parts that weren't intended
to be funny and cry at parts that were. They may overrate
the movie as they automatically fill in the gaps that nobody
else could. Or they may underrate it because, as my friend
said about *The Count of Monte Cristo,* they know the film-
makers changed the ending and left out the most important
parts.

If a teacher movie were ever made that would completely satisfy teachers, the public would find it utterly
unwatchable. It would send the general moviegoer out
of the theater midway through, screaming "No more! No
more!" Teachers know that the only way a movie could ever
even come close to capturing what teaching is really like
would be if it were about seventeen hours long—and you
weren't allowed to leave to go to the bathroom.

So even though I will continue to wait for a genuine teacher movie, I still obsessively watch any type of movie or TV show about teaching. In addition to the movies already mentioned, I've seen *Up the Down Staircase, Teachers, Lean on Me, Conrack, Dead Poets Society, The Substitute, The Faculty, Kindergarten Cop, Mr. Holland's Opus, High School High,* and *The Principal.* I even sort of liked the made-for-TV movie *To Sir, with Love II,* with Sidney Poitier coming out of retirement at the age of seventy to teach at an inner-city school in Chicago.

Though teacher movies are oversimplified, misleading, and occasionally insulting, I figured out why I continue to watch them. If you have ever had the opportunity to watch a movie that was filmed on location near where you live, you might have enjoyed it for the same reason. During the movie, you might have poked the person sitting next to you, presumably your friend, and proudly said, "That's my building," or, "I've been to that deli! They've got great potato salad."

Part of that is what I like about teacher movies. They remind me of where I've been. I also get a cheap thrill out of knowing that "I was there," at a place worthy of being in a movie—the classroom. For that reason, I will keep watching every teacher movie that gets made. Except maybe *To Sir, with Love, III.* Even I have my limits.

I also get a cheap thrill out of knowing that "I was there," at a place worthy of being in a movie— the classroom.

Voices from the past

It's always a thrill to hear from former students, and I'm sometimes surprised by what they're up to and why they've chosen to contact me.

Everyone who goes into teaching has the same goal: to make a difference. But it is usually impossible to measure how much of a difference we make. There are the small day-to-day differences like a student acing an exam, but the long range differences are a lot less obvious. We assume that we're making them, but the only way to be sure is if, years later, students actually contact us.

Because of the advent of e-mail and social networking sites like Facebook, I'm part of the first generation of teachers to have the opportunity to hear from a large number of former students on a regular basis. It's always a thrill to hear from former students, and I'm sometimes surprised by what they're up to and why they've chosen to contact me.

The first ever to contact me was a girl named Jennifer who was in my class during my fourth year of teaching. By that time in my teaching career, I was feeling pretty comfortable with the students and had shed my robotic personality enough to occasionally joke around. In Texas, the big standardized test students had to take was then called the Texas Assessment of Academic Skills, or TAAS. Jennifer's note reminded me that while our school was preparing for this test, I had created a bunch of somewhat inappropriate, but funny, motivational buttons that students proudly wore around school. Here's what she wrote:

...I thought about you the other day when I found my senior memories book that has your famous "Kick some TAAS!" button in it. I would love to know how you're doing lately....

Occasionally, I will receive e-mails that make me think that maybe, just maybe, I wasn't as bad as I thought I was during those first years:

...You were one of the handful of teachers that really impacted my life. I saw how much you really cared for the students and I could tell how much you loved teaching. Your class was always very informative and fun.

Olga and Felipe. During my second year of teaching, I visited the middle school I had left in shame after my first dreadful year. It was nice that some of the kids seemed genuinely happy to see me. There were two awful moments, however.

One was when two of the students I had struggled with my entire first year teamed up to embarrass me. One crawled behind me while the other tried to push me over him. Somehow I managed to stay standing—a sort of symbolic reminder of my entire first year.

The most disappointing moment of the homecoming, however, was my meeting with Olga, the top student from my first year. Despite my awful classroom management, Olga had managed to get an average of 110. She did equally well in all her classes and was named valedictorian of her class that year. I felt close to Olga, and at the end of the year, she said something unusual to me that I've never forgotten:

You know when I knew that you respected us? When that girl hit you in class and you didn't hit her back.

But at that reunion visit, one of my old students said to me, "Did you see Olga?"

The most disappointing moment of the homecoming, however, was my meeting with Olga, the top student from my first year.

I also remembered him for the many cartoon drawings he had done of me during that first year. Most of them depicted scenes of me yelling at kids.

"No," I said. "Why?"

"Olga's bad now," she said. "She's dating Herman." Herman was one of the students who had been expelled the year before for hitting me.

I found Olga sulking in front of the school. Before I even got a chance to say anything, she looked at me and said, "What?" Even though I was really nothing to her, a teacher she'd had last year, I tried to counsel her. I said something like, "Olga, you're too smart to be like this." She shook her head and walked away. I was nothing to her.

The next time I would see Olga was four years later, in 1997. I was visiting the area, and a friend of mine at the high school sent a note to all my former students that she could find. She told them they could meet me in her office after school.

The first student to come down was a boy named Felipe. One of my best students during my first year, he would nod his head in approval anytime I seemed to be on the verge of gaining control. I also remembered him for the many cartoon drawings he had done of me during that first year. Most of them depicted scenes of me yelling at kids. He didn't know it, but I saved most of them as proof for anyone who didn't believe what I went through in my first year.

A few more kids came in to say "Hi," and Olga was one of them. She was back on track, and just as my poor teaching had nothing to do with her losing her way in seventh grade, my pep talk, I'm sure, had nothing to do with her recovery. She gave me her address and asked if I'd write to her.

Here is an excerpt from my letter:

I guess you're a senior now, which is really amazing since it doesn't feel like that long ago that you were a sixth grader in my class. I'm sure you realized that was not a very good year for me. I had just graduated college two months before and was only 21 years old on the first day of school that August. In what was certainly the most difficult year of my life, I learned more about teaching than most people do in ten years.

After that year, I started working at a high school, where I was very successful, never yelling again. After my fourth year of teaching, I was even awarded the Teacher of the Year at that school. Of course, all the awards in the world will never take back the fact that I really did you and your classmates an injustice by making all those mistakes my first year, and by losing control of my classes so quickly. When I last saw you, it seemed like you were doing well and have recovered from any damage I inflicted through my incompetence that year...

In 1991, at times when I really wanted to quit teaching, it was students like you and a few of your classmates who inspired me to stay. I knew that maybe you were one of the only ones following along. I had to cover so much material so quickly, as I didn't have much time after spending the first 20 minutes of each class yelling at kids and sending them to the office.

Though that year was just one of thirteen years of schooling for you, and probably not very memorable, for me that year will never be forgotten as it was my first year working, and also because it was so difficult for me.

> *Looking back now, I see that I was begging for forgiveness.*

Looking back now, I see that I was begging for forgiveness. She didn't write back. It would be another ten years before I heard from her again.

161

Ten Years Later

Students become teachers. Eleven years after that visit to his high school, Felipe, now 27, e-mailed me. I wrote back and told him about what I had been doing and that I'd had a book published about my experiences teaching him and his classmates.

He wrote back:

I'm glad we had the opportunity to find each other again after so many years. I remember you being a good teacher, I mean I think you knew a lot about math and I could understand you. I also remember you shouting at the others all the time, especially Jose. There is or was a drawing or picture of some sort, I'm not sure if I had anything to do with it or maybe I drew it or something but it showed you screaming. Do you remember that or is that something I'm creating in my mind of the vague memories I have? I just want to say, way to go, I'm proud of you and I'm glad you were my teacher. I'm glad that it all worked for you, I remember thinking, "Man, this guy is not going to make it, he's going to quit." I was glad to hear that you hadn't quit when you came to see us in high school. And now you've written a book about it, that's pretty cool! I think I'm going to have to buy it and read it because I've been thinking about becoming a teacher.

Not only did I remember that picture; I still had it!

Not only did I remember that picture; I still had it!

I will teach dis' class if I hafta'!

Sadly, during my first year of teaching, students spent a little too much time drawing unflattering pictures of me.

It was his idea of a career change that prompted Felipe to contact me. He wanted advice about what he should say in his upcoming interview. I guess he figured that even if I wasn't much of a first year teacher, I did get a job so I must know something about getting through an interview. He also mentioned that Olga was in his teacher training class.

A few days after my conversation with Felipe, I got an e-mail from Olga. She wrote:

Teaching was so stressful that it was giving him high blood pressure.

> *Hi, Mr. Rubinstein! I don't know if you remember me, but ironies exist and I am a teacher. Felipe gave me your address and so I wanted to contact you. My life has been a roller coaster full of many highs and lows. I wish I could talk to you, you always understood. Anyway, this whole teaching thing is overwhelming and I have had my doubts. I need a lot of advice and sadly not many people can give it. I hope we can start some type of communication. Where are you now? What is going on with you? Hope to hear from you soon.*

I called Olga and we had a long conversation about teaching and about life. She had battled a lot of problems, but she had persevered and was excited about her new career. Finally able to teach her something without getting interrupted every five seconds, I gave her the advice about classroom management that I've been working on for all these years.

I was happy that these two former students had become teachers, and I had been excited to hear from them. However, a month after Felipe started teaching, I got an e-mail from him saying that he had quit. Teaching was so stressful that it was giving him high blood pressure. Believe me, I felt his pain.

Olga was struggling too, but she seemed like she was going to make it.

Meeting in person. In 2008, I went back to the area where I'd had my first teaching experience. In preparation of my trip, I e-mailed every student I had heard from and invited them to an informal reunion at a bar. (They were all around 30 years old by then.)

At the reunion, nobody seemed to know what had happened to Sarina.

It was great to see the former students who wanted to come and see me. But missing from the reunion was Sarina, the class clown I had enjoyed so much. I had lost touch with her about five years earlier. At the reunion, nobody seemed to know what had happened to Sarina. They had heard that something bad had happened, though they couldn't remember if she had died or was in jail, but it was something.

About six months later, I was thrilled to get an e-mail from Sarina that said, "I finally caught up with you. I would like to hear from you." I wrote back right away and told her about my life and sent her pictures of my newborn daughter. She wrote back:

> *I was elated to hear from you and your daughter is gorgeous. Glad she didn't take after you...hahaha. Well I'm just trying to get myself together after the storm, its pretty bad but I'm making it. Well, you and your family take care until I hear from you again. Love ya.*

She never told me what the "storm" was, though I get short friendly e-mails from her sporadically.

Perhaps the most exciting e-mail I've gotten from a student was from Olga after she completed her second year of teaching. She forwarded me something from her principal, informing her that she was voted Teacher of the Year at her school. Maybe her front-row seat view of my horrible first year taught her a little about how to avoid the most common teacher mistakes.

But I like to think the copy of *Reluctant Disciplinarian* I sent her had helped a little, too.

Maybe her front-row seat view of my horrible first year taught her a little about how to avoid the most common teacher mistakes.

Acknowledgments

I would like to thank a number of people who were instrumental in the production of this book:

- Cheri Thurston, my editor, for her patience and for believing I had something important to write.

- Robin Milanovich, for her friendship and support while I wrote much of this book.

- My sister, Jani, for our brainstorming sessions.

- Wendy Kopp, for founding Teach For America.

- My teacher friends who contributed to the final chapter.

- My friends who wouldn't let me quit during my first year, especially Jon Fish and Armando Alaniz.

- All the teachers who ever taught me.

- My first year students. I'm sorry I didn't allow you to shine. Perhaps what you taught me about teaching will now help other teachers to succeed.

About the author

After graduating from Tufts University in 1991, Gary Rubinstein trained as a teacher with the Teach For America (TFA) program, which recruits recent graduates to teach in rural and inner-city schools throughout the country. During his five years with the program, he taught both middle school and high school students and wrote a monthly TFA newsletter column called "I Didn't Do Nuthin'." During his fourth year, he was named Teacher of the Year at the high school where he taught.

Gary Rubinstein frequently speaks at conferences, workshops, and teacher trainings. If you would like him to be a part of your next event, e-mail garyrubinstein@yahoo.com for more information.

He currently works at Stuyvesant High School in Manhattan. He has trained teachers for Teach For America, the New York City Teaching Fellows, and Math For America. His essays and articles about teaching have appeared in national magazines and journals, including *Education Week*, *Teacher Magazine* and *Mathematics Teacher*. He is a two-time recipient of the Math For America Master Teacher fellowship. He lives in New York City with his wife Erica and daughter Sarah.

Rubinstein and his daughter Sarah. Will his techniques work with a toddler?

Before

Gary Rubinstein as a student teacher in 1991

After

*Five years later, Rubinstein as a teacher
(Back then you could get a lot more glasses
for your money!)*

*Rubinstein dances with student
Sarina Holmes at the senior prom.*

Rubinstein meets with former students in 2008.